I0480669

CHOICE HACKING

HOW TO USE PSYCHOLOGY AND BEHAVIORAL SCIENCE TO CREATE AN EXPERIENCE THAT SINGS

JENNIFER L. CLINEHENS

For my incredible fiance Rob, who inspires me everyday to be the best I can be xxx

For my parents, who always buy my books even though they have no idea what they're about :)

And for all the people who've helped develop Choice Hacking through reading, giving feedback, and lending praise.

Thank you all for supporting this book!

WHEN YOU FINISH READING...

Thank you so much for reading *Choice Hacking*!

If you read the book and enjoy it, please consider leaving a review with your favorite book retailer or Goodreads.

Reviews are a huge help for independent authors because it helps us find new audiences. We really need and appreciate the support. Thank you!

DON'T FORGET YOUR FREE
COMPANION COURSE

While you're reading, don't forget to check out the FREE Choice Hacking Companion Course.

You can learn more and sign up at ChoiceHacking.com/CompanionCourse101.

The free course includes:

- Bonus real-life examples and use cases
- Bonus video content
- Resources and links mentioned in the book
- Downloadable worksheets

Tap to get free access to your bonus material now: ChoiceHacking.com/CompanionCourse101

HOW TO DESIGN AN IRRATIONAL EXPERIENCE

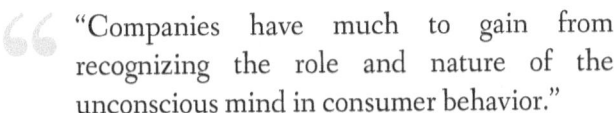 "Companies have much to gain from recognizing the role and nature of the unconscious mind in consumer behavior."

— Philip Graves, author of Consumerology

Primed by a pandemic

Like everyone on Earth, you've heard the word "coronavirus." Not only have you heard it, but experts have debated it, scientists have analyzed it, and some people have panicked over it. Coronavirus is a deadly disease that transformed the world overnight, so, understandably, the word has been at the tip of everyone's tongues. Because of the similar-sounding names, the media naturally became curious if it would impact Corona beer sales. So they asked. And customers responded that yes, they intended to stop buying Corona beer. In fact, 38% of Americans[1] said they would not buy Corona beer "under any circumstances." But in reality, people were saying one thing but doing the opposite. While customers were saying they'd never buy Corona again, sales quietly grew 28.8% by April 2020[2].

On the surface, Corona beer and coronavirus have nothing in common other than their first three syllables. But the mere mention of coronavirus triggered unconscious associations with a cold, frosty beer. How is it possible that a deadly pandemic could drive beer sales? And why were customers saying one thing while doing the exact opposite? It's down to the irrational ways the environment influences human behavior - the field of behavioral science.

———

Behavioral science: what it is and how to use it

Behavioral science explores why people behave the way they do. Itself a subset of psychology, behavioral science includes two broad sub-categories:

- **Information sciences:** This is the study of how humans take in information and how it affects their decision-making and behavior. Research comes from disciplines like cognitive science, neuroscience, and neuromarketing. Areas of practice that could apply this research include information architecture, store merchandising, personalization algorithm design, experience design, store design, and marketing.
- **Relational sciences:** The study of how human decisions and behavior are affected by social interaction. Research originates from sciences like sociology and social psychology.

Within experience design, affected disciplines might include the design of social media platforms, gamification, store design, loyalty program design, and more.

For the purposes of *Choice Hacking*, I consider principles fair game so long as they've been stress-tested and peer-reviewed in a research environment. To be considered, the principle must deal with how people behave, make choices, and consider information.

What you need to know about how people think

The last 50 years have seen leaps forward in our understanding of how the brain operates. The work of researchers like Daniel Kahneman, Amos Tversky, and Richard H. Thaler have transformed the fields of economics, consumer behavior, and psychology.

Before Kahneman and Tversky, scientists and economists thought of people as "Homo Economicus" - a species that behaved rationally, methodically considered choices, and were reasonable decision-makers. But as we'll find out in *Choice Hacking*, the "Homo Economicus" doesn't exist in the real world. Richard H. Thaler, behavioral economics pioneer and the author of *Misbehaving: The Making of Behavioral Economics*, put it this way:

 "The purely economic man [the so-called "Homo Economicus"] is indeed close to being a social moron. Economic theory has been much preoccupied with this rational fool."

Decades of scientific research was based on this nonexistent, rational person. But pioneering work by Kahneman and Tversky started a paradigm shift regarding human decision-making. This new school of thought is based on the following principles:

1. Everyone is irrational
2. People don't know what actually motivates them
3. Everyone uses mental short cuts to make decisions

1. Everyone is irrational

As we'll explore, one of the defining characteristics of humans is that we behave irrationally. There is no situation in which people *objectively* weigh all the variables of a decision before acting. Bias, assumptions, and mental shortcuts all play a part in how we evaluate choices. In his book *Predictably Irrational: The Hidden Forces That Shape Our Decisions*[3], researcher Dan Ariely described irrationality this way:

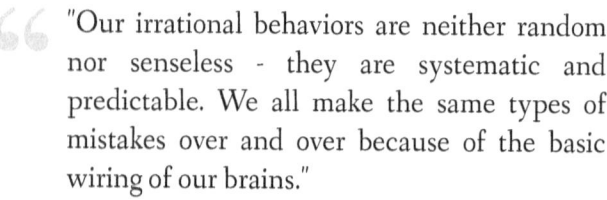

"Our irrational behaviors are neither random nor senseless - they are systematic and predictable. We all make the same types of mistakes over and over because of the basic wiring of our brains."

As Ariely says, even though people behave irrationally, it's still possible to predict how they will react to a given situation. In *Choice Hacking*, we'll explore common irrational behaviors and how we can apply their predictability to create experiences customers will love.

2. People don't actually know what motivates them

At the core of behavioral science is the idea that people aren't aware of what's driving them. We're all more influenced by our choice environment than we realize.

For example, The Anchoring Effect states that people use the first piece of information they see to judge later information. This principle was explored in a study by research duo Amos Tversky and Daniel Kahneman.

Participants watched a roulette wheel that was rigged to stop only on the numbers 10 or 65. They were then asked to answer a seemingly unrelated question, guessing the percentage of the United Nations members that were from Africa. If subjects saw the roulette wheel stop on 10, they guessed a number that was 25% lower than people whose wheel stopped at 65.

What the participants didn't realize was that the "random" number on the roulette wheel had influenced their answer to an unrelated question. As this study showed, people greatly underestimate context in their decision-making. Also known as the fundamental attribution error[4], it's a key principle of behavioral science and one of many we'll discuss in *Choice Hacking*.

3. Everyone relies on mental shortcuts and biases to make decisions

In the past, scientists not only assumed that people act rationally but they also assumed what we think rationally as well. What we now know is the brain works in a so-called dual process manner. In the dual process model, the brain uses two kinds of thinking - fast and slow:

- Slow thinking is the type you'd use when writing an essay or composing a symphony. It's deep work, contemplative and methodical. Above all, it's hard work. The type of work our brains want to avoid because it consumes a lot of time and physical energy. In short, our brains are lazy, and slow thinking is hard.
- Fast thinking, on the other hand, is off the cuff. It relies on biases and mental rules of thumb, called heuristics, to make 95% of our decisions. Our brains prefer this type of thinking because it's easy and doesn't take much time.

I'll reference this quote several times in *Choice Hacking*, but I love it because of how well it illustrates the brain's bias toward laziness:

 "Thinking is to humans as swimming is to cats; they can do it but they'd prefer not to."

- Daniel Kahneman

How can we apply behavioral science to the customer experience?

If you work in experience design, you've likely run across psychology or behavioral science terms. In fact, there's become a bit of a buzz around them over the last decade. They've been talked about a great deal though their application to the experience has been pretty sporadic. In *Choice Hacking*, we'll learn to apply science to the customer experience in a systematic manner. You'll discover that by leveraging these principles, your work will be more robust and your recommendations more effective.

Defining the "customer experience"

The customer's experience is such a big concept that we'd be well served to define it before we begin. For the purposes of this book, we consider the mechanical, social, transactional, and emotional experiences of a brand. Digital and physical touchpoints are both covered, such as websites, store designs, and mobile experiences. *Choice Hacking* also touches on out-of-home, digital, and video advertising although they aren't the focus of this book.

Because the purpose of many experiences is to drive sales, we will also explore how to tie the advertising environment to the customer experience, ensuring consistency between all touchpoints. *Choice Hacking* may challenge you to look beyond your realm of expertise, but I'd encourage you to stretch your thinking.

With that in mind, there are a few ways we can apply behavioral science to the customer experience, as we've just defined it.

1. Create effective touchpoints (including advertising)
2. Design a choice environment that gets people to buy
3. Manage emotional responses to and memories of the experience

The beautiful and sometimes challenging thing about applying behavioral science is that it can work well in literally millions of moments, and on many different levels. It's not as cut and dried as it may first appear, and our improvements come in the form of increasing the probability that customers will take action.

1. Create effective touchpoints

On every level of the customer experience, we can use behavioral science to inform the purpose and design of our touchpoints. For example, at a high level, we can use research to inform the purpose, context, and content of touchpoints throughout the customer journey. We'll answer questions like:

- How can we use the information on earlier touchpoints to influence decisions at later touchpoints?
- How critical is a specific moment in the journey to a customer's memory of the experience?
- How do we know if customers are noticing what we're telling them?
- An understanding of what types of messages are best suited to which part of the customer journey.

We can also use behavioral science and psychology to go a layer deeper and inform the details of a specific touchpoint, answering questions like:

- How many steps should we have in our checkout process?
- In what order do we show products in a suggestive sell process?

- What color buttons do we use on our webpage?

2. Design a choice environment that gets people to buy

A choice environment, sometimes called a choice architecture, is the way we present a choice and how this presentation influences behavior. When you apply behavioral science to the design of a choice environment, you increase the probability that customers will do what you want them to.

You no longer have to rely on gut feel or questionable qualitative research to make design decisions. Instead, you can base your approach on proven, peer-reviewed research and rigorous experimentation. For example, you can use behavioral science to inform:

- How many product options to show to drive sales.
- How to price each product so that customers view them in context, and choose the "right" product.
- How to frame promotions so that they drive sales.

3. Manage emotional responses to and memories of the experience

Before you think *Choice Hacking* is all about the mechanics of selling, know that behavioral science can drive brand love as well. Our judgments, memories, and behaviors are profoundly affected by our emotional states. That's why a compelling customer experience must manage actions *and* emotions.

The psychologist Jonathan Haidt used the metaphor of a man riding an elephant to describe the relationship between our emotional and rational brains: the elephant is our emotions, and the rider is our rational mind. The rider might look like they're in charge, but when there's a disagreement between them, the elephant usually wins. When we use behavioral science to manage customers' moods and memories, we're more likely to persuade them to take the "right" actions as well.

An example of how moods affect decision-making was shown by researchers[5] who wanted to know if people in a good mood would be more likely to help a stranger than someone in a bad or neutral mood. They put a quarter clearly visible in a phone booth and waited for someone to find the coin. Then, an actor working for the research team, interrupted by asking to make an urgent phone call. The people who saw the coin, happy with their sudden good fortune, were more likely to allow the actor to cut in front of them in line.

Can we prove that behavioral science will improve customer experience?

When you're designing or improving experiences, there are many tools you can use to drive change. How do we know that behavioral science will make an impact?

The consulting firm McKinsey[6] ran a study looking at experience improvements at a consumer-services firm. They tested improvements in both operations and through applying behavioral psychology principles. The firm found that using behavioral psychology raised satisfaction scores 56.25% more than operations improvements alone.

Additionally, behavioral science initiatives have been rolled out in many different sectors, including government. The British Behavioral Insights (B.I.T.) team inside the U.K. government created £100M of financial return based on a cost of only £520k[7].

Behavioral science initiatives, when carefully and correctly integrated, can make a massive difference in both the public and private sectors. When using a proven approach, applying science to your experience can have significant upside.

Behavioral science is for everyone

Before you say, "This is great, but now I'm worried. I should consult an expert before I experiment with behavioral science," you should know that applying these principles isn't just for researchers. In fact, people doing experiments "in the field" have an advantage - customers behave more naturally. Yes, you'll have challenges regarding distractions and other uncontrollable factors. But that's because it's the real world, not a lab. Once you finish *Choice Hacking*, I'd encourage you to try applying behavioral science. As long as you're honest with customers, it's hard to imagine a downside to creating a better experience.

CONTENTS

THE C.H.O.I.C.E. MODEL

WHAT MAKES AN EXPERIENCE GREAT?

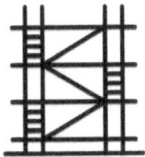

"All models are wrong, some are useful."

- George Box, statistician

The story of C.H.O.I.C.E.

The idea of a behavioral science model is not new. After the book *Nudge: Improving Decisions About Health, Wealth, and Happiness* was released, designers and marketers began applying behavioral science and psychology, but often without a systematic approach. Behavioral insights have also been used by governments for years to improve public policy design and implementation. For example, in the United Kingdom, the government's Behavioural Insights Team (B.I.T.) designed a model called E.A.S.T. It explains how to frame communications to drive customer action. The acronym stands for:

- Make it easy
- Make it attractive
- Make it social
- Make it timely

E.A.S.T. is a proven framework for government and social services work. But E.A.S.T. wasn't designed for customer experience. That's why I've created the C.H.O.I.C.E. model. It's a bespoke model created to apply psychology and behavioral science to the customer experience. After a decade of designing digital and physical experiences for brands like AT&T, Adidas, and McDonald's across four continents, I've battle-tested which behavioral science and psychology principles are most effective in practice. C.H.O.I.C.E. is purpose-built for those who manage, design, and implement user and customer experiences.

The Elements of C.H.O.I.C.E.

Best-in-class experience should include each one of the elements below. One might be weighted more heavily than another, depending on the brand and its touchpoints. But a leading experience implements each of these elements in some way. They are:

- **Clear**: Is your experience salient and simple for people to understand?
- **Holistic**: Does your "big picture" experience set up individual interactions to succeed?
- **Open**: Does your experience make it clear what's happening now, why, and what's to come?

- **Individual**: Does your experience use relevant data to personalize?
- **Contextual**: Does the context of your experience subtly guide customer choice?
- **Emotional**: Do customers have positive emotions and memories associated with your experience?

How to use the C.H.O.I.C.E. model

C.H.O.I.C.E. lays out the components of effective experiences. In each section of this book, we'll examine the psychology and behavioral science behind every element and how you can implement each. You can also use the C.H.O.I.C.E. model to:

1. Structure your thinking

Are you being asked to create a new customer experience? There's no need to start from scratch. Use C.H.O.I.C.E. to help you understand what elements to consider, which questions to ask, and how to apply specific principles to create an effective experience.

2. Analyze your journey to find areas for improvement

C.H.O.I.C.E. can be used as a scorecard for continuous improvement, to pinpoint problems when an experience is broken, or as an additional section on a customer journey map. Ask yourself, are we delivering all of these elements?

3. Defend strategic and design decisions to clients

You can also use C.H.O.I.C.E. for supplemental strategic support to defend UX and design decisions. For example, a pitch for a new app may have been built with best-practice, but not driven by a specific strategy. The C.H.O.I.C.E. model can help you support best practice design principles with scientific reasoning, to create a stronger overall pitch to clients.

The C.H.O.I.C.E. Model in Action

In the later chapters of this book, we'll breakdown how three leading brands - Uber, Disney, and Netflix - apply the C.H.O.I.C.E. model. By working through real-life examples, the applications and benefits of this model will become more clear. Now, on to the elements of C.H.O.I.C.E.

PART ONE
CLEAR

IS YOUR EXPERIENCE SALIENT AND SIMPLE FOR PEOPLE TO UNDERSTAND?

"Designers love subtle cues, because subtlety is one of the traits of sophisticated design. But users are generally in such a hurry that they routinely miss subtle cues."

— Steve Krug, author and designer

What is a "clear" experience?

Clear experiences are easy to notice and easy to navigate. These experiences make it clear to customers what actions they need to take and how. People live in a noisy world, with lots of information competing for their attention. These distractions mean our brains prefer simple, conspicuous messages. As Steve Krug put it, "Don't make me think."

ONE

CLEAR: SALIENCE BIAS

PEOPLE CAN ONLY USE INFORMATION THEY CAN NOTICE

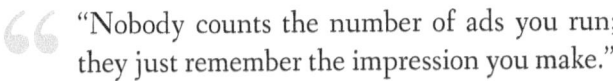 "Nobody counts the number of ads you run; they just remember the impression you make."

– Bill Bernbach, founder of advertising agency DDB

The operations team at Schiphol Airport in Amsterdam had a problem. No matter how many times a day the janitorial team made the rounds, the men's urinals were always a mess.

As many a mother, partner, and bathroom floor can attest, men often lack "urinary precision". In public toilets, the mess caused by hundreds of misses can be unsanitary and expensive to clean. Schiphol Airport solved their problem with a simple but brilliant solution. They placed an etching of a fly inside each urinal bowl.

These tiny engravings were incredibly effective at reducing the mess. The flies reduced spillage by 80% and total cleaning costs by 8%. As Klaus Reichardt, a member of the team who invented the solution, put it[1]:

"Guys are simple-minded and love to play with their urine stream, so you put something in the toilet bowl and they'll aim at that.

It could be anything. I've seen a golf flag, a bee, a little tree. It just happens that at Schiphol it's a fly."

But why did such a simple solution work so well? It's down to a behavioral science principle known as salience bias.

Salience describes how prominent or emotionally striking something is[2]. If an element seems to jump out from its environment, it's salient. If it blends into the background and takes a while to find, it's not. Salience bias states that the brain prefers to pay attention to the salient elements of an experience[3]. But what makes something salient?

Salience works by creating what's called cognitive ease[4]. This concept means making it easy for people to process information, which in turn makes the experience clear. But to do that, we need to know what visual elements make something salient. They are luminance, texture, contrast, and scale.

1. Luminance

Luminance is the intensity of light emitted from an object. For example, a glowing effect around an element will make it stand out from its background.

2. Texture

Textures are patterns that add more visual information. Any type of angular or interesting texture attracts attention.

For example, fried chicken is more salient than grilled chicken because its crunchy texture draws attention.

3. Contrast

Contrast is how different two colors are to one another. For example, black text on a yellow background is a combination often used for road signs. Yellow contrasts with the surrounding environment, and black contrasts with the yellow background. This results in a clear message that's also easy for drivers to notice.

4. Scale

Scale is the relative size of one element in comparison to another. In some cases, a client's request to "make the logo bigger" is correct, at least when it comes to salience.

The context of a customer's experience will affect how likely they are to find an element salient. For example, if you were to walk into a new grocery store, with crowded aisles that had no clear system, and no signs, how easy would it to find batteries? Even if the battery display used luminance, scale, contrast, and texture to stand out, you'd still have a hard time finding it. That's because the context of the experience isn't salient, therefore the product is even less so.

In retail and digital experiences, the salience of products can be manipulated by changing where and how they're shown. For example:

- **Product convenience:** A 2012 study found that when compared to having water on just one big shelf in a store, adding lots of smaller baskets of water bottles near different types of food increased their salience. Making water more convenient and therefore more salient boosted sales by 28.5%[5].

- **The complexity of a digital or physical store experience:** Researcher Barbara Kahn highlighted the need to make stores easier to navigate[6]. In her 2017 study, Kahn suggested that a reduction in product options and a simplification of the amount of information that's presented can have incredible effects on sales.

- **Easy to scan shelves:** Product displays make a big impact on customer engagement. In a 2014 study, a research team collaborated with brands like H&M and IKEA to study the effect of product displays on intent to buy[7]. They found when products were arranged vertically by type (for example, a column of red towels versus a row of red towels) there was a 90% increase in customers picking up and inspecting the items.

Not only can the shopping environment affect salience, but a person's emotional, mental or physical state can as well[8]. For example, when you're thirsty you're more likely to notice an ad for Coca-cola. You're also more likely to remember an experience that is highly emotional, and thus more salient[9].

How to apply salience bias to your experience

The purpose of an experience is to drive customer action. Here's how the best brands use salience to shape their customer experience:

1. Apple: Keep it salient by keeping it simple

Ruthlessly product-focused, Apple stores set the bar for simple retail experiences. Rather than confusing customers with lots of information and options, Apple lets its products persuade.

Their product-first strategy is also clear in Apple's digital experience. Simple design and minimal information make it easy for Apple's products to get 100% of the customer's attention.

2. Netflix: Create clarity from complex information

Customers love Netflix because it has lots of content, but having lots of content means it can be hard to find what you want. Netflix's UX team has a difficult job—they have to turn this endless content into an easy-to-navigate experience. Here are a few ways they accomplish this:

- **Content personalization algorithm:** Research has shown that personalized content is more salient to customers. Netflix describes itself as "customer-obsessed" and strives to deliver a totally personalized experience. Their *"Top Picks"* category is a prime example of this philosophy in action. In fact, more than 80% of Netflix shows[10] customers watched in the last two years have been as a direct result of Netflix's recommendation engine. Not someone searching for a specific piece of content.

- **Top 10 lists:** Netflix leverages the "Top-10 Effect" in its new, content ranking section. This effect states[11] that people naturally group things into round-number groups, and everything outside of these groups is inferior. In other words, top 10 lists are incredibly salient for customers—they naturally grab people's attention.

The bottom line

 "Salience is the biggest part of the job."
—Mark Ritson, journalist and marketing professor

Clearly, salience is one of the most important elements when designing customer experiences. We can use it to make better design decisions and create more effective experiences.

But measuring salience objectively can be difficult for designers. Some design best practices will result in a salient experience. But the time it takes to create something makes it hard to empathize with a customer who just scans a poster or a page on a website (if they see it at all).

Luckily, there's been a recent boom in salience tools that use AI and algorithms to model human attention. Salience tools are used in digital design and are being adopted in advertising and customer experience as well. But iterative design practices, while not as objective as an AI tool, can also create salience.

TO APPLY SALIENCE BIAS, ask yourself:

- In key moments in our customer journey, what's the *one action* we want customers to take? Is there any information we need from them before they can move on? How obvious have we made this requirement? Can we use customer data to pre-populate this information?
- Do we need to land any specific information about our product? If so, are we relying on words or visuals to tell the story? Are our visuals focused and simple?
- What's the context of our physical experience? Is it vying for too much of our customer's attention? For example, in a retail experience are the merchandising elements too brightly colored? Do they compete with our products for the customer's attention?
- What's the context of our digital experience? In a digital experience, do we have irrelevant information or too many design elements? Is display advertising or additional product marketing taking away from our ultimate strategic goal, such as selling the product?

TWO

CLEAR: THE SIMPLICITY THEORY

WHY PEOPLE PREFER SIMPLE EXPERIENCES

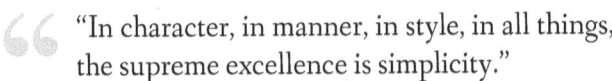 "In character, in manner, in style, in all things, the supreme excellence is simplicity."

— H.W. Longfellow, poet

An increasing demand for people's attention has combined with endless options to create a noisy and crowded environment. To complicate matters, there are more dimensions on which to judge an experience than ever before. Even a task as simple as buying a bag of coffee has dozens of elements on which to judge your options - blend, roast, sustainable farming practices, organic or non-organic, origin, and grind. Going to the supermarket means the complex process of choosing one product has to be repeated dozens of times each trip.

This complexity has ramifications for both businesses and customers. Brands have to work harder to standout from their competition. And when it comes to standing out, most brands' instincts are to do, offer, and shout about *even more "stuff"*. Customers, who as we've established don't want to think, have to take on more decisions every day.

There are no silver bullets in business. Success is a combination of internal and external factors. But there is one principle that the most-loved brands share — a simple experience that's easy for customers. And the more complex the world gets, the more people crave simplicity.

The Simplicity Index[1], created by consultancy Siegel+Gale, is a yearly ranking of brands with the least complicated experiences. Siegel+Gale's research has produced some compelling insights about the impact of simplicity.

1. **Simplicity drives love**. According to their research, 64%[2] of consumers are more likely to recommend a brand because of a simple experience.
2. **Simplicity drives growth**. Since 2009, a stock portfolio made up of the simplest publicly traded brands (as defined by Siegel+Gale) has outperformed the market by 686%[3].
3. **Simplicity drives sales**. 55% of consumers are willing to pay more for uncomplicated experiences.

The underlying psychology of why simplicity is so appealing is called the simplicity theory[4]. This theory states that people have a bias toward simplicity and are predisposed to choose products and experiences that minimize their cognitive load. In other words, simple experiences make people think less. As John Collard of Yale University said,

> "Not only is it hard work to think, but many people fear the activity itself.
>
> They are docile and obedient and easily follow suggestions put forward by others because it saves them the labor of thinking for themselves."

But what do we mean when we say "simplicity"?

Calling something simple is like calling it beautiful — the specifics can be hard to nail down. What's simple to one person might be complicated to another. But in Siegel+Gale's research, there are three basic tenants that all of the industry-leading experiences share:

1. Get the basics right

Simple experiences deliver on their brand promise. They don't confuse customers with hundreds of combinations of offers; they deliver what customers came for quickly and easily.

2. Provide tangible value

No customer cares if you offer a simple experience but don't provide something they need. Each of these brands is a master at building products and services that customers are willing to buy, repurchase, and recommend to their friends.

3. Keep the experience transparent

The best experiences are honest. They don't confuse customers with complicated pricing, rely on random promotions, or hide critical information.

So which companies have the simplest experiences?

1. Netflix

Netflix's simplicity lies in the service it provides and the experience that it creates.

 "Whether you're vegging out at home or aboard a cross-country red-eye, hosting your own personal Bill Murray retrospective or rewatching all 10 seasons of *Friends* is as easy as reaching a device, opening an app, and pressing Play.

The platform takes ease of experience one step further, with algorithms that track your viewing patterns, eliminating the arduous decision-making process of what to watch next."

- Siegel+Gale Simplicity Index, 2019

When you subscribe to Netflix, there's no doubt you'll get exactly what you paid for - a personalized streaming service that "just works". Its marketing is upfront about their cost to value tradeoff. Netflix may raise their prices, but they'll never have blackout periods for comedies or charge overages for binging *The Office*.

Personalization also helps make their experience simple. But consider the Netflix catalog. In 2020, Netflix had 5, 838 selections available in the U.S.[5] down from a peak of 11, 000 titles in 2012. If the site were just a portal for thousands of TV shows and movies with no personalization, customers would feel overwhelmed and anxious. There might be a "new" section or different categories. But the experience of choosing and watching a title is subjective, emotional, and highly personal. The Netflix personalization algorithm helps customers find something that they'll enjoy, and eliminates the pain of digging through thousands of titles. Not to mention that a movie that's a bad match for a customer's individual taste also gives that person a bad experience. It's in both Netflix's and the customer's interest to serve up the right content to the right people.

2. ALDI

When it comes to simple experiences, it's hard to beat German grocer ALDI. Their stores double down on fundamentals, in service of Aldi's unique brand proposition of fast, cheap, and high-quality food. Walking in, you're greeted by product displays best described as bare-bones - cardboard packing boxes sitting on plain metal shelves. There's no on-shelf advertising aside from the price and product packaging, and no cluttered end-aisle displays. All of the information Aldi presents in their stores is simple, straight forward, with no over-the-top sales language.

Aldi's products are mainly generics, with a twist. Store items have names that make it obvious what "real brands" they represent. Instead of Honey Bunches of Oats cereal, there are Honey Crunch n' Oats. Their take on Oreos are called Borneos, and so on. Even the packaging designs make the experience fast and easy. On every Aldi-produced product, the UPC that cashiers use to ring-up products appears on every side of the package. That way, cashiers don't waste time searching for the code on every product. Siegel+Gale summed up Aldi's experience this way:

> "... Aldi understands the real path to its shoppers' hearts is a stress-free, no-frills shopping experience. People credit the German brand for helping them 'save time' as well as its 'reasonable prices.'
>
> Simple, consistent floorplans plus uncomplicated offers, high-quality products, and excellent customer service, proves that Aldi is determined to give value back to its loyal customers."

3. Google

The simplicity of Google's search experience is what continues to differentiate them from competitors. The iconic Google search box, sitting alone on a white background, hasn't changed much since it launched in 1998. Although the search graphic itself now changes for holidays and to recognize cultural events, the simplicity of the search experience remains. Siegel+Gale described it this way:

> "While it's a radically different world since its launch 20 years ago, Google hasn't strayed from its original mission... the universally 'accessible' brand soldiers on, pushing the

boundaries of available technologies to organize the world's information."

The bottom line

Putting simplicity into practice can be difficult to achieve. Embedded processes, established ways of working, middle managers looking for ways to justify their roles, organizational structures, and lack of market orientation all make it difficult to create simple experiences[6]. As Dan Gingiss wrote in *Forbes*[7],

 "Simplicity is a basic tenet of customer experience, but it is often overlooked in favor of a company's outdated rules or procedures."

TO APPLY THE SIMPLICITY THEORY, ask yourself:

- Where do we see customers getting frustrated in our experience? This might be indicated by dwell time, drop-off, or autonomic research that indicates frustration and anger.
- If we look at our competitors' experiences and compare them to ours, who has the most simple experience? Is this reflected in our sales or brand perception?
- Are there ways to move a process from the customer-facing "front stage" to the internal "back stage"? In other words, could employees, digital platforms, or machine learning simplify the customer experience?

THREE

CLEAR: CHOICE OVERLOAD AND THE CHOICE PARADOX

PEOPLE WANT CHOICES, JUST NOT TOO MANY

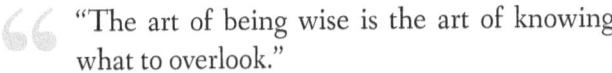 "The art of being wise is the art of knowing what to overlook."

— William James, psychologist and philosopher

We often assume that giving people more options is better. The conventional wisdom says that lots of choices will empower customers and make them feel more confident about their final decision. But in reality, more options can be paralyzing. The conventional wisdom regarding options is both correct and incorrect. Research says that there is a delicate balance between too much choice and not enough. Too much choice will overwhelm, but just enough will drive sales - a principle known as the choice paradox.

For example, in a famous study[1] conducted at Columbia University, a research team set up a booth of jam samples. They stood in a store and waited for potential customers to sample, and possibly buy, jam. Every few hours, the researchers would switch from a selection of 24 jams to a group of six jams. The team wanted to see how the availability of choice affected customer behavior, and whether more or less choice would result in additional sales.

When there were 24 jams on display, 60% of customers would stop to get a sample, and 3% of these customers would buy a jar. So all in all, not a stellar conversion rate. However, when there were six jams on display, only 40% stopped. So when there was more choice, more people were attracted to the display. Here's the interesting part about the display with fewer options — 30% of these people bought jam. So if 100 people passed by the booth, 1.8 of them bought a jar of jam when there were 24 choices. When there were only six choices, 12 people bought a jar of jam. The takeaway? Lots of options attracted customers to browse, but fewer choices got them to buy.

The negative effects of choice can be more severe than a missed sale. Research shows that when there are too many options, customers feel anxious, will disengage, and can even become depressed[2]. It's the idea that while some choice can be good, too much choice will overwhelm. How satisfied someone is as compared to the number of available choices can be described by an inverted "U" model. Having no options makes customers unsatisfied. Having more options lead to more customer satisfaction at first. But at a certain point there are just too many choices to consider - customers begin to feel confused and dissatisfied with their final decision. This effect is known as choice overload.

Introduced in the 1970s by futurist Alvin Toffler in his book *Future Shock*[3], choice overload has implications for every business and customer experience. In fact, according to research from Episerver[4], 46% of customers have failed to complete a purchase online due to overwhelming choices. A brand's good intentions - giving customers lots of options - can backfire and become a barrier to sales.

So how do we decide how many options to show? In his book *The Paradox of Choice*[5], Barry Schwartz starts by outlining the steps of decision making:

1. Figure out your goals
2. Evaluate the importance of each goal
3. Array the options according to how well they meet each goal
4. Evaluate how likely each of the options is to meet your goals
5. Pick the winning option

What makes a buying decision easy? The key is keeping the cognitive load - how much thinking we ask customers to do - low when comparing features. If you make customers think too hard, they'll give up to avoid the process altogether. If features in a choice set aren't easy to compare, or are hard to find, the decision becomes more difficult. For example, if I ask you to compare an iPhone and a Samsung phone by telling you that one has 16 GB of data and the other has 10 GB of data, that's an easy comparison. But if I tell you one has 16 GB of data and the other can hold six million photos, the choice is much harder.

The more options you have overall, the harder it is to make a comparison across products. You'll always feel like you've missed out on crucial information. If the brand asks customers to compare choices across 50 dimensions instead of 3, they'll feel like they might miss out on "the one." And that's the paradox. Having a variety of options is good. It drives customer consideration. But once the number of choices gets too high, a person's satisfaction with their decision goes down.

The curse of too many options

When your experience provides too many options, you risk creating something too complex to convert. This choice overload not only lowers the chances customers will buy but can have psychological implications as well.

1. Anxiety

Too much choice is the cause of mental anguish for some people. Economist Herman Simon theorized that decision-making styles fall into two types:

1. Satisficers: People who would rather make an "ok decision" than the perfect decision. They've spent some time considering their options, but haven't belabored the process. They tend to be more satisfied with their choice because they don't consider all the available information.

Satisficers settle for an option that's "good enough" and move on. Gretchen Rubin, author of "The Happiness Project" described them this way[6]:

> "Satisficers make a decision once their criteria are met; when they find the hotel or the pasta sauce that has the qualities they want, they're satisfied."

2. Maximizers: These are people who want to make the best decision. They can't choose until they've deeply examined every possible option.

Research from Swarthmore College[7] found that Maximizers reported significantly less life satisfaction, happiness, optimism, and self-esteem. They also experienced much higher levels of regret and depression than Satisficers.

2. Disappointment

The more options people have, the more likely they are to be disappointed in their choice[8]. You never feel that you made the best decision because there were too many options to consider.

As Barry Schwartz writes in *The Paradox of Choice*[9]:

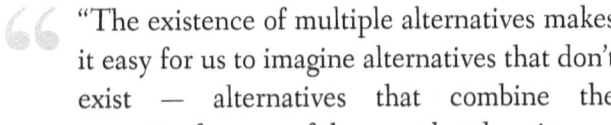

"The existence of multiple alternatives makes it easy for us to imagine alternatives that don't exist — alternatives that combine the attractive features of the ones that do exist.

And to the extent that we engage our imaginations in this way, we will be even less satisfied with the alternative we end up choosing.

So, once again, a greater variety of choices actually makes us feel worse."

So how do we combat choice overload in our customer experience?

1. Offer fewer options

It may seem counterintuitive in the age of personalization, but options need to be limited to maximize sales. For example, Procter & Gamble found[10] that a decrease in the number of Head & Shoulders varieties resulted in a 10% increase in revenue.

To find the right amount of choice for your experience, a combination of analysis and experimentation is critical. You may find that there are efficiencies that your product team would love to make already, or that a particular product doesn't return an optimal amount of margin. Before killing off products or options completely, experiment with showing fewer choices. Measure sales, engagement, and satisfaction with real customers before committing to which options to remove.

2. Make it easy to compare features across products

If you want to make it easy for customers to choose between non-equal options, frame the use of each. For example, software company Calendly uses Basic, Premium, and Pro options arranged in a simple to read table to reduce the number of choices. Then, they compare individual features across products in a table that's clear and easy to digest. Now instead of feeling confused and anxious about which version to pick, customers can easily choose the product that's right for the features they need.

The bottom line

Because business has a bias for action, it's common to see brands undermine their good intentions when it comes to choice. But it you reduce the number of options available, you also reduce complexity for the customer, your product teams, and the business overall. In the end, it's this reduction in complexity that will smooth the way to increased consideration, higher engagement, and more sales.

. . .

TO AVOID CHOICE OVERLOAD, ask yourself:

- Where are the critical decision points in our experience, and where do customers seem to be confused?
- Are there any points in our experience where customers think they're spending longer than they are? Research shows that the amount of choices and the perception of time are related[11]. The moments where customer perception of time doesn't match the reality are key indicators for choice overload.

PART TWO
HOLISTIC

DOES YOUR "BIG PICTURE" EXPERIENCE SET UP INDIVIDUAL INTERACTIONS TO SUCCEED?

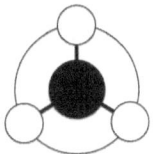

"The trick to forgetting the big picture is to look at everything close up."

— Chuck Palahniuk, author

What is a "holistic" experience?

A single touchpoint never works in isolation. Individual moments interconnect in ways that are bigger than the sum of their parts. Designing a holistic experience means considering the moments before and after a customer interacts with your experience, and how this psychological context can set up your digital and physical touchpoints to succeed or fail.

Think of the three behavioral science principles in this section like steps in a process. The aim of the process is to create a holistic experience where everything interconnects. A holistic experience sets the stage for interactions for success, such as ordering food on your app, or returning a pair of shoes that didn't fit. These key moments and principles are:

1. Becoming a customer's first choice before they know they need your product - the mere exposure effect.
2. Getting people ready to buy, through influencing the final moments before they make a choice - the priming effect.
3. Molding a customer's opinions of your brand, by assuring them they've made the right choice - confirmation bias.

In each step of this process, we will pull different levers to influence customers.

In step one, mere exposure, we will use our brand's unique visual language, also called brand symbols or semiotics, to become top of mind with customers. The elements of this visual language could include a logo, a distinctive color, or even a jingle or a unique sound.

In step two, priming, we will learn how to design the sensory environment surrounding a choice. We will consider how the sights, sounds, smells, and words we use can set up our touchpoints for success.

In step three, confirmation bias, we'll learn how customers consider information differently after they've made a choice. We will learn how to use the sensory environment, communications, and interaction elements to assure customers that the choice they've just made is the right one.

FOUR

HOLISTIC: THE MERE EXPOSURE EFFECT

PEOPLE PREFER THINGS THEY LIKE, AND THEY LIKE THINGS THE MORE THEY SEE THEM

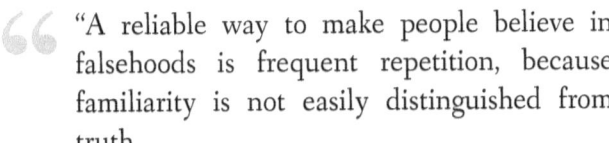

"A reliable way to make people believe in falsehoods is frequent repetition, because familiarity is not easily distinguished from truth.

Authoritarian institutions and marketers have always known this fact."

- Daniel Kahneman, psychologist and Nobel laureate

Every brand wants to be the top of mind choice for their customers. If you are, when the moment comes to buy, you're the first place they visit. But even if you're pouring millions of dollars into advertising, getting noticed isn't easy. In a 2004 study[1] by Yankelovich Partners, researchers estimated the average customer saw up to 5,000 ads a day. Compare that with the 1970s, when a person only saw about 500 advertisements every day. Given the amount of competing information people are exposed to, how can you break through? Behavioral science points to one key principle that gives companies an edge in the fight for attention. It's called the mere exposure effect.

Coined in the 1960s by social psychologist Robert Zajonc, the mere exposure effect states that when people are familiar with something, they prefer it[2]. And given a choice of two options, they'll choose the one they've been exposed to the most, even if it's lower quality.

For example, a 2012 study of the Eurovision song contest discovered an interesting connection. The number of times an audience saw a contestant correlated with how many votes the contestant received. It didn't matter if the contestant wasn't a great performer. As long as they were seen more often, the contestant received more overall votes[3]. Just like the Eurovision voters, customers prefer something the more they see it. And the more they prefer something, the more likely they are to buy it.

The mere exposure effect is best applied before people realize they need your product. Think about the brand "Masterclass". It's an online course catalogue where leaders in their field, like actor Samuel L. Jackson and chess master Garry Kasparov, teach their process. If you used the internet this year, chances are you saw what felt like a thousand Masterclass ads. They popped up before YouTube videos and in the middle of blog posts. Affiliate marketers wrote about them and they took over display ads. In short, they were everywhere.

You may have found yourself, like myself and many others, hating the Masterclass ads at first. They were overexposed and repetitive. But eventually, they started to become a little more interesting and entertaining. Like me, you may have become less and less annoyed by DeadMau5 talking about electronic music. You may have even joined Masterclass and learned a thing or two. That's mere exposure at work. Here's more examples about how the effect can help set your experience up for success:

1. Mere exposure can drive desire

This effect can be a powerful persuasion tool, but not in the way you'd expect. According to Zajonc, the effect can take place subliminally, and that's when it's most effective[4].

Communications don't have to be noticed to have a powerful effect on a customer's behavior — just being exposed is enough. For example, researchers at Princeton University published a study[5] in which they added a subliminal message to an episode of The Simpsons. The team inserted 12 frames of the word "thirsty" and 12 frames of a Coca-cola can. Their subjects couldn't guess what had been added since the frames went by too quickly for people to notice. But people rated themselves 27% thirstier after watching the show.

2. Mere exposure can drive preference

Subliminal messages not only drive customer need but can also drive brand preference. Research exposed subjects to subliminal images of Lipton Iced Tea. They found people were then more likely to chose Lipton when presented with a choice of drinks[6].

In channels like out of home, video, social and TV, communications can drive a need. If your marketing creates a connection with your brand's visual language, customers will start to associate their need (thirsty) with your brand experience (Lipton Iced Tea). For this to be effective, there are two guiding principles to keep in mind:

1. Communications must be single-minded and image-driven
2. For mere exposure to work, there must be visual consistency across touchpoints

1. Communications need to be focused and image-driven

Each touchpoint must be focused on one message or task to be effective. If we try to give customers too much information, they'll become overloaded and tune out.

Images act as the glue between the "pre-experience" and individual touchpoints, driving connections between a customer's need state (thirsty) and the product (Coke). Brand codes - assets like logos or colors - can etch themselves in people's minds. By using these images over and over we establish a visual language for our brand. Semiotics, the study of signs and symbols as a means of communication, has proven that the repetitive use of images can improve the persuasion ability of any communication[7]. When we use these codes to connect the "big picture" to our individual interactions, our experience will be more successful.

2. For mere exposure to work, there must be consistency in communications

Having too many images or ideas in your communications can undermine your touchpoings. Not only does it waste money, but it can actually work against your experience in the long run. That doesn't mean you can't have fun with your brand codes in a way that is both interesting and consistent. Some brands, like McDonald's, Coca-cola,

Target, and Mastercard, have mastered reworking their brand codes so that customers can remember them more easily.

For example, when Coca-cola turns their logo's white ribbon into two people holding hands for World Peace Day, they're playing off of customers' existing knowledge of their logo. Coca-cola is also grabbing attention with a new take on a familiar image. Customers understand that this is an artistic improvisation of the Coca-cola logo, and it cements the logo more firmly in their minds.

Mere exposure is a powerful principle that can work across any part of the customer journey, including advertising, retail and digital experiences. If connected to individual interactions, it can be a powerful preamble to your experience. Make sure to align marketing messages across touchpoints, and vary the core message and visuals as little as possible. Creating a consistent pre-purchase experience that clearly flows into touchpoints is vital for mere exposure to work.

If you are managing individual touchpoints or digital experiences, you can connect to the pre-purchase communications in several ways. For example:

- Use product recommendation engines that show more of the same brands in which customers have already, and in which they've shown an interest. If we know this customer already has affinity for a specific brand, showing it more will increase their likelihood to purchase. And their affection for this brand will translate to liking our experience more.
- Consider relying on well-worn conventions of digital design. For example, placing the

company's logo on the upper left hand side of the page, or using standard icons such as an envelope for email. When an experience is familiar, customers will prefer it.

- Create email drip campaigns that reiterate your message and improve familiarity with your company. If you can keep contact with your customers by giving them something of value, and remind them of your brand, you can create more affinity.

The bottom line

In the end, customers trust what they already know. Getting them to know you takes time, money, and consistency in message. If you confuse them with too much information, or too much variation, you won't be able to work a groove into their memories because your message is constantly changing.

TO APPLY the mere exposure effect, ask yourself:

- Are we sending a consistent message across every touchpoint or user flow in the experience?
- Are we including clear branding across every touchpoint, so customers understand that it's our brand?
- If not, how can we simplify and focus our creative, to take full advantage of the effect?

FIVE

HOLISTIC: THE PRIMING EFFECT

PEOPLE'S UNCONSCIOUS MINDS INFLUENCE MOST OF THEIR BEHAVIOR

 "The main moral of priming research is that our thoughts and our behavior are influenced, much more than we know or want, by the environment of the moment.

Many people find the priming results unbelievable, because they do not correspond to subjective experience. Many others find the results upsetting, because they threaten the subjective sense of agency and autonomy.

If the content of a screen saver on an irrelevant computer can affect your willingness to help strangers without your being aware of it, **how free are you**?"

- Daniel Kahneman

First demonstrated in the 1970s, priming is when our brains call on unconscious connections in response to a stimulus, also called a prime[1]. In other words, what we're exposed to now changes our behavior later.

Priming is passive, subtle, and people aren't aware it's happening. And it can be activated with almost any kind of stimulus. Images, words, smells, light, sound, tasks, touch, or temperature can all unconsciously affect our choices. As long as someone has an existing association with one of these stimuli, it can affect their judgment and behavior.

In a holistic experience, priming sets the stage for action. It can get customers ready to buy, make a particular decision, develop an opinion about a product, or evoke an emotion.

Consider the case of Marmite. After the United Kingdom voted to leave the European union, Marmite, a brand of spreadable yeast extract, got into a public price dispute with a major British grocer, Tesco. Marmite, driven by supplier price increases due to the so-called Brexit vote, asked Tesco to up their on-the-shelf price by 10%[2]. Tesco refused, and a disagreement ensued.

The spat with Tesco severely damaged customers' perception of Marmite. Their reputation scores declined by 11.6 points, and purchase intent dropped -3.9 points[3]. But because of the press generated by Marmite's public fight with Tesco, sales of Marmite increased by 61%.

Why? Because when customers heard the word "Marmite" over and over, despite the context, they were primed to buy the brand. So when they went to the supermarket, customers were unconsciously driven to choose Marmite. Not because they were persuaded by an ad, but because the news coverage primed their subconscious minds to buy.

There are six kinds of environmental primes

Because priming draws on subconscious associations, it can be triggered by any number of stimuli. For example:

1. Priming with images

The most common type of priming used by marketing and advertising firms, priming with images uses visuals to create associations and trigger behavior. When designing a physical or digital experience, you can also use images to prime behavior, decisions, and perceptions.

For example:

- People will behave more creatively when they're primed with the Apple logo. When primed with the Disney logo, they're more honest[4].
- Women can be primed to feel more confident when giving a speech, if they are primed with a photo of a powerful woman, such as Hillary Clinton[5].
- Brand codes - the colors, logos, shapes, and sounds that make up a brand - can be unconsciously primed. For example Marlboro were prohibited by European law to display the logo of their cigarette company on the race car it sponsored. Marlboro used priming to its advantage by applying a sly red and white paint job to their Formula 1 car. When the car was in motion, the paint blurred just enough to look like the Marlboro logo. This way, the company was able to prime customers and stay on the right side of the law - at least for a little while.

2. Priming with light

It turns out, there is some truth to the saying "good lamps are the best police". In a series of three experiments, lighting conditions were shown to vastly affect participants' behavior[6]. People in darkened rooms are more likely to cheat on a test. According to one study[7], 61% of people in a dimly lit room cheated, but only 24% of people cheated in a brightly lit room.

3. Priming with smells

Interestingly, smell has proven to affect whether customers will buy a product, and how much they'll pay for it.

- Psychologists at a university in the Netherlands found that when students were primed with the smell of lemon-scented cleaner, they were more likely to clean up after themselves when given a snack[8].
- A study conducted by researcher Alan Hirsch found that gamblers played 45% more at slot machines when the room was filled with a "pleasant smell" than when no smell was added[9].
- In another study[10], Dr. Hirsch found customers would pay $10 more for a pair of Nike tennis shoes in a flower-scented shop. 84% of the subjects also said they were more inclined to buy the sneakers in the scented room.

4. Priming with words

In several studies, researchers found that priming with words related to either credit cards or cash can have huge effects on customer behavior[11].

For example, they found that:

- Priming subjects with words related to credit cards can cause them to focus on the benefits of a product as opposed to the costs.
- Another study found that those primed with credit cards responded faster to the benefits of an iPhone than those primed with cash. They were also prepared to pay more for the phone ($205) than the cash prime group ($163).
- In an additional study, people were primed with credit card concepts or cash concepts. Researchers then asked participants to choose an MP3 player. Either an expensive iPod, or a Zune which was much cheaper and had fewer features and benefits. 76% of those in the credit card prime group chose the iPod. But, only 25% of the cash prime group chose the iPod. Most of them went for the Zune.

5. Priming with touch and temperature

People's behavior can even be influenced by heat, cold, texture or weight.

- A Yale University study showed[12] that holding a hot or cold beverage before an interview could change the opinions about the interviewee.

- Another study found that the weight of objects can affect the perception of importance[13]. Subjects were asked to answer a survey about whether various public issues should get more funding. The heavier the clipboard, the more money the person felt should be allocated to the cause. The hypothesis being that the metaphorical weight of the issue was primed by the physical weight of a clipboard.

6. Priming with sounds

Music and auditory feedback can influence our perceptions of an experience. For example, a study by Massimiliano Zampini and Charles Spence found that people think chips are fresher if their bite is accompanied by a loud and satisfying "crunch" sound, even if the chips are stale[14].

Three things to keep in mind, when applying priming to your customer experience

1. Priming must be subconscious

As Nobel laureate Daniel Kahneman wrote:

> "An effective prime needs to be strong enough to impact behavior, but not so strong that it enters conscious thought — the effect must remain subconscious."

In other words, it can't be obvious to customers that

they're being primed, or the effect doesn't have the same power. This obviously brings some ethical considerations to bear when applying priming. Please read chapter twenty-two, "Hidden Dangers of Behavioral Science", to learn more about ethical priming.

2. You can leverage unconscious and aspirational brand associations

With the proper application of priming, you can amplify existing mental associations.

For example, a restaurant chain that wants to be seen as healthier could consider adding fresh fruit as a side in all of their ads. An athletic shoe brand could pump the smell of fresh-cut grass in their stores to evoke running through sports fields in spring. Ask yourself: What are the association we want customers to make with our brand?

Consider which primes that could stimulate these unconscious associations, and experiment with how and where to use them.

3. Priming works best in people who already care about the thing being primed

In 2016, Professor Dolores Albarracín at the University of Illinois at Urbana–Champaign conducted a meta-analysis[15]of "priming" research papers. She focused her analysis on finding smaller effects on people who already care about the thing being primed.

Albarracín found that people who want to become thinner are more likely to make healthy food choices if they are primed with "thin" words. But if the subject doesn't care about watching their waistline, the priming effect was not nearly as strong.

In any discussion of priming, it's worth noting that much of the initial research in this field has recently been subject to intense scrutiny. Specifically, the repeatability of certain studies has been called into question[16]. However, the general principle of priming has retained merit.

When applying a behavioral science principle, it pays to approach applications with a skeptic's mind. Always keep up with the latest developments in the field, and experiment with small applications before applying these principles to large parts of your business.

The bottom line

When considering how to prime customers, we need to be clear on both the decision points in our experience and the pre-decision points. In other words, what are we priming customers to do? Only when we understand the connection points can we find the perfect moments to prime.

TO APPLY THE PRIMING EFFECT, ask yourself:

- What are the key moments in our customer journey?
- What are the emotions we want customers to experience during these key moments?
- What are the actions or choices we want people to take at these key moments?
- What goals do most of our customers share when interacting with our business? How can

we make sure we're priming to those who can actually be primed?

- What's happening just before these key moments in the experience? Are there touchpoints or a user flow that we can use to prime our customers in an ethical way?

———

SIX

HOLISTIC: CONFIRMATION BIAS

PEOPLE'S DESIRE TO BE RIGHT INFLUENCES THEIR MEMORIES, ACTIONS, AND BELIEFS

"Believing is seeing... once we have a belief, we see the information that will confirm that belief, and we stop seeing what we don't want to see.

- Dr. Carol Tavris, social psychologist

Have you ever ordered dinner in a restaurant, and after telling the waiter your order they comment "Good choice!". How did it make you feel? Did you begin looking forward to your meal a little more, knowing that your decision was a "good" one?

If so, you're not alone. When taking a risk, making a choice, or buying a product, people love to hear that their decision was a good one. So much so, that they'll ignore information that directly conflicts with this belief. Why? It's an example of a psychological phenomenon known as confirmation bias.

Coined by psychologist Peter Wason, confirmation bias describes peoples' tendency to search for, interpret, favor, and remember information that confirms their choices and beliefs[1]. As author Harper Lee put it,

 "People generally see what they look for, and hear what they listen for."

For example, when a customer decides to buy something, they are more open to information that confirms their purchase was high quality, healthy, a good value, or environmentally sustainable. Customers want to believe they've made the right choice, so communications that support that belief are well-received and better remembered. So how can we apply this principle to the customer experience?

Confirmation bias can be applied to any phase of the customer journey. But the best time to use it is after customers have made a decision or a purchase. That's because confirmation bias can be used to create positive memories of an experience.

Why are post-purchase moments so powerful? It's down to another behavioral science principle known as the peak-end rule. We will explore this rule more deeply in chapter seventeen, but at a high-level this rule states that people judge an experience based on how they felt at its peak and its end. They don't judge the experience by the average of every moment. And when customers have better memories of an experience, they're more likely to recommend and repeat it.

Best-in-class brands know that confirmation bias is a critical psychological tool when creating customer experiences. Three brands that demonstrate how best to apply this effect are Mailchimp, Pret a Manger, and Holiday Inn Express. Here's how they apply confirmation bias to their experiences:

1. Show your users some love, like Mailchimp

A list of customers' email addresses is one of the most powerful assets a business can leverage. People who want to see your marketing messages in their inbox have incredible sales potential. So it's no surprise that one of the most nerve-wracking things a small business or startup can do is send an email out to its list.

Every time a company presses "send" on an email, they risk damaging their reputation with a mistake or losing customers forever if they unsubscribe. Mailchimp, a popular email service provider, knows this feeling well. As Aaron Walter, Director of User Experience at Mailchimp put it[2]:

 "I became a Mailchimp customer in 2005 and I knew the feeling of sending out a campaign and being totally stressed out about it. Because once you send an email, you can't really suck that back in.

I just always thought, 'Someone should come into my office and high five me right now! I'm deserving.'"

It's this insight into customers' mindsets that spawned a gif of an animated monkey giving users a high-five. The gif appears right after customers have sent an email, and taken a huge risk. At that moment, customers need confirmation that they've made the right choice. And that's exactly what Freddie, Mailchimp's cartoon monkey mascot, gives them.

In fact, Freddie's high-five has become so powerful that it's actually spawned a subbrand, complete with merchandise. And according to the blog *Inside Design*, Freddie's high-five is now one of the "most cited examples of user empathy"[3].

2. Reconfirm a customer's choice with quality messages, like Pret a Manger

Pret a Manger is a fast-casual sandwich shop located in nine countries[4] across Europe, Asia, and North America. A brand that prides itself in serving natural and organic food quickly, Pret isn't shy about showcasing their quality ingredients.

What's interesting about Pret's experience is how many messages in the seating area tell simple stories about food quality. Many fast-casual restaurants would spend this post-purchase time trying to talk customers into buying more food. But Pret knows that post-purchase is the best time to talk about their natural and organic ingredients.

Pret's customers have made a decision and taken a risk on Pret because they feel it has good quality natural and organic food. By applying confirmation bias during this time in the journey, Pret is reconfirming that their customers have made the "right choice".

3. Call attention to what makes your experience amazing, like Holiday Inn Express

When Holiday Inn Express launched its SimplySmart bathroom makeover, it believed it had created something special[5]. High-powered showerheads by Kohler, upgraded linens, and a curved shower rod that created more space for bathers were just a few of the innovations in which the brand invested millions.

But the challenge of telling customers about these

upgrades, without boring them to death, was real. When booking a budget hotel, how many of us make our decisions based on a point-by-point comparison of the bathroom features? Instead, we make a decision by recalling our last visit, or going on the word of a friend.

Often the last thing people do before checking out of a hotel is spend a lot of time in the bathroom — showering, blow-drying their hair, and using the hotel soaps and lotions. And as we know from the peak-end rule, time at the of an experience is disproportionately important.

Knowing how critical the end of the guest experience is, Holiday Inn Express created signs in their rooms and bathrooms detailing the SmartShower, and calling attention to the upgrades. The copy on the signs was evocative. For example, when describing the new showerheads, the signs read:

> "Sleek, stylish brushed chrome finish, three powerful spray settings, and a unique pressure compensating flow regulator that automatically adjusts to keep water pressure strong and steady."

By pointing out all of the things that the showerhead was doing well, customers began to notice and believe Holiday Inn Express. Customers began thinking to themselves, "The showerhead did seem really nice, and the towels were fluffier than normal. Hey, I made a pretty good choice when I picked Holiday Inn Express. Good job me!"

The bottom line

Confirmation bias can be a powerful and surprisingly emotional tool to use when designing customer experiences. Although it can be applied anywhere in the journey, using it after customers have made a purchase or taken a risk will help ensure their memories of the overall experience are good.

TO APPLY CONFIRMATION BIAS, ask yourself:

- Where are the moments in our customer journey where customers have made a decision or purchase? Are there any specific product attributes we want to reconfirm at that time?
- Is our product or experience a risky one? How would customers feel if we gave them a virtual pat on the back?
- How can we be more empathetic toward customers after they've taken a chance on our experience? Can we show our appreciation or call attention to some extra effort we've put into elements of our experience?

PART THREE

OPEN

DOES YOUR EXPERIENCE MAKE IT CLEAR WHAT'S HAPPENING NOW, WHY, AND WHAT'S TO COME?

"You know you're not anonymous on our site.

We're greeting you by name, showing you past purchases, to the degree that you can arrange to have transparency combined with an explanation of what the consumer benefit is."

- Jeff Bezos, founder of Amazon

What is an "open" experience?

Companies often assume customers aren't interested in what happens "behind the scenes". Others may not want to be upfront about how their products are made. But modern customers are savvy and care deeply about issues like sustainability, fair labor practices, and how their data is used. Their expectations for transparency are high.

An "open" experience is clear about what makes it

special. It provides a look behind the scenes at all the right moments, and drives value by being upfront about issues customers care about. An open experience also lets customers know where they stand and what's expected of them. However, an open experience doesn't mean that customers need to see everything. Instead, brands with open experiences understand that there's much to gain from giving customers more of the "right" information.

SEVEN

OPEN: OPERATIONAL TRANSPARENCY

PEOPLE VALUE EXPERIENCES MORE WHEN THEY GET A PEAK "BEHIND THE SCENES"

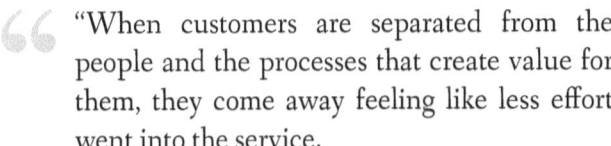 "When customers are separated from the people and the processes that create value for them, they come away feeling like less effort went into the service.

They appreciate the service less and then the value the service less as well."

— Ryan Buell, Harvard Business School

Have you ever eaten at Subway Sandwiches? Their servers, called Sandwich Artists, make your food to order right in front of you. Step-by-step you tell the Artist what you want and how much of it you'd like, and they construct your perfect Subway sandwich. "Showing their work" has proven to a be compelling business proposition. Subway is one of the largest food franchises in the world, with more than 41,000 stores in 100 countries[1]. Subway leverages the power of a principle called operational transparency to drive love for their experience.

Operational transparency is the inclusion of windows into your company's process so customers can see the effort that's going into their experience. According to recent research[2], experiences that use operational transparency cause customers to value products more highly[3] and can even make people happier[4].

An example of operational transparency in action is a study about its impact on college cafeteria workers and the students they serve[5]. In one scenario, the cafeteria was set up much like a Subway restaurant with the cooking process visible to students. In the second scenario, the cooking process was hidden in a separate kitchen. When students could see people making their food, they were able to make a more personal connection, not just to the servers, but to the process of creating meals. As a result, they rated the quality of the food 22% higher. There was a similar effect on workers who could see the students they were serving. In fact, output went up 19%. By making a connection with students, the cooking process became more personal for the workers as well. They cared more when they could make a connection with the benefits of their labor.

Brands with industry-leading experiences often feature operational transparency. Here are a few brands that have created big impact by applying the principle:

1. Dominos Pizza

Back in 2008, Dominos had a big customer experience challenge. When a customer's order took longer than expected, they'd call the store on the phone to see where it was. This would cause a chain reaction . The employee on the phone would put the customer on hold, go back to the kitchen, talk to the staff and interrupt the pizza-making process. This disruption would cause operational chaos and delays for everyone.

Dominos knew they had to do something to stop customers from calling the store. They soon realized there was already a system they could use to improve transparency — their order management software. This internal software was used to create the Dominos Pizza Tracker, which shows customers exactly what's happening with their order. They can watch as their pizza moves through the "prep", "bake", "box", and "delivery" phases. The Pizza Tracker not only improved Domino's customer experience by giving a peek into the process, but kept store operations running smoothly as well.

2. The City of Boston

Cities all over the world struggle with street maintenance. Many times, it's so busy fixing the old problems that it doesn't keep an eye on new ones that are developing. To manage this challenge, Boston built a website[6] where residents can report potholes and track the repair process online. By showing people what's happening behind the scenes, the city is able to reduce duplicate complaints, or requests for follow-up information.

The program was such a success that the service can now be used for a litany of complaints. Snow shoveling, overflowing trash cans, and sign damage are all handled through the service. There's even a 3-1-1 app[7] that anyone can download to take pictures and make reports on the fly.

3. Tessei

Tessei is a Japanese company that cleans bullet trains. They transformed customer perceptions of their company by applying operational transparency. Cleaning work wasn't respected because it was perceived to be dirty, dangerous, and difficult. Teruo Yabe, a company leader, thought if the process was more transparent, customers might change their perceptions. Yabe knew he had to make cleaners more salient so people would notice them. He changed the color of employee uniforms from a pale blue that was hard to spot while crews were cleaning, to a bright red.

Called the "Seven-minute miracle"[8], customers can watch 22 people clean a thousand seats in only seven minutes. This simple visibility fundamentally transformed the dynamic between cleaners and customers. What had been perceived as a shameful job in the past, was now one to which people began to aspire.

The bottom line

When customers respond to transparency, what they're really engaging with are the people that deliver the experience. It's the human side of a brand experience that makes it so compelling. The more we automate the customer experience, the more we need to consider how we show this transparency. AI, chatbots, and automated checkouts can all provide operational efficiency, but we have to make sure they're delivering operational transparency as well.

TO APPLY OPERATIONAL TRANSPARENCY, ask yourself:

- Can our customers see, speak to, or interact with our employees? Can customers watch the labor process? Is there a way to make our employees centerstage in the customer experience?

- Do people know where our products come from, and how they're made? Can we provide any more information on how their product is being assembled while they wait, or before they've seen the item on the shelf? Can we provide pictures or other visual confirmation? What parts of the process do our customers care the most about? Examples might include Fair Trade practices or sustainability initiatives?

- When customers are waiting for a delivery, are we clear about where, when, and how this is being fulfilled? Is it clear to them what "late" looks like and are we communicating to them why a package might need to be delayed? Have we considered how to make the returns and complaints process an opportunity to delight our customers?

EIGHT

OPEN: THE GOAL GRADIENT EFFECT

GIVING CUSTOMERS VIRTUAL GOAL LINES WILL INCREASE THEIR MOTIVATION AND ENGAGEMENT

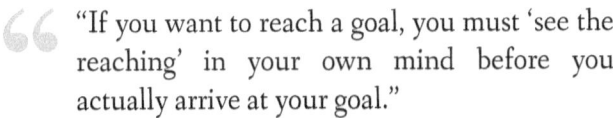 "If you want to reach a goal, you must 'see the reaching' in your own mind before you actually arrive at your goal."

- Zig Ziglar, author and speaker

Coined by behaviorist Clark Hull in 1932, the goal gradient effect states that as people get closer to a reward, they speed up their behavior to get to their goal faster[1]. In other words, people are motivated by how much is left to reach their target, not how far they've come. As Hull put it in his original research:

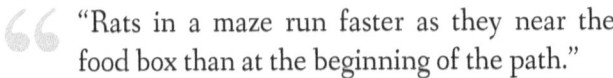 "Rats in a maze run faster as they near the food box than at the beginning of the path."

The closer customers get to their goal, the more encouraged they become to finish. But they can't get motivated if they don't know where the finish line is. For this reason, you'll often see the goal gradient effect at work in gamification elements like progress bars, badges, and profile completion percentages. It can be applied anywhere users are encouraged to complete a big task by achieving smaller objectives. Some examples of brands that apply the goal gradient effect to their experiences include:

1. Duolingo: Use "chunked" progress bars to drive engagement

Duolingo, the language learning app, is a master of using the goal gradient effect to keep people engaged. Every section of its material is broken down into smaller subsections, each with its own mini progress bar. This approach to language learning combines the goal gradient effect with chunking, a psychological learning technique. Chunking is a process by which big groups of information - the Spanish language, for example - are broken down into smaller parts. Then these parts are grouped by common elements. In the case of Duolingo, it chunks subjects into smaller topics like "Family," "Time," and "Sizes." The app then applies the goal gradient effect to show users exactly how much they have left to do before completing each subsection. The subsections feed into bigger sections, and before long the user has learned a new language.

2. LinkedIn: Use progress bars to drive profile completion

One of the most common applications of the goal gradient effect is in interaction elements that show progress, such as the "Profile Strength" feature on LinkedIn. This feature clearly shows how complete a user's profile is, and how much further they have to go before completing it. LinkedIn gives users a name for their progress, such as "intermediate" which provides more clarity about where they are in the process. By combining a progress bar with a measure of completeness, LinkedIn makes it easy for customers to know where they stand. For added measure, they've combined the goal gradient effect with data to persuade users that their work will help them be "discovered in search by recruiters." The goal gradient effect helps LinkedIn users feel like the finish line is closer than they may think.

The goal gradient effect can drive loyalty as well as engagement. Researchers Kivetz, Urminsky, and Zheng[2] conducted a series of field experiments involving coffee loyalty programs. Customers were given coffee punch cards, and researchers observed their behavior. They found that customers would buy coffee much more frequently the closer they got to their free coffee. Based on this research, the team developed the endowed progress effect. This principle states that if you give people a bit of fake progress toward a goal, they're much more motivated to achieve it. For example, if you've ever been to a coffee shop where the barista gave you two stamps instead of one, you've experienced the endowed progress effect. The research team also tested the Endowed Progress Effect in a car wash. In that case, loyalty cards given extra stamps by the team were redeemed 34% of the time, versus only 19% redemption for cards where no extra credit was given.

The bottom line

The goal gradient effect is a useful tool to drive customer engagement in both physical and digital experiences. If you're looking for places to apply goal gradient, think about where customers tend to drop off in your experience.

. . .

TO APPLY the Goal Gradient Effect, ask yourself:

- Have we included visual representations of a customer's progress in our experience? Are there enough badges, progress bars, and other gamification elements?
- When we remind a customer that they've left something in their cart, does our language reflect how close they are to completing their goal? For example, "You're almost there, only one more step!"
- If we have a loyalty program, what would be the effect of seeding the first few purchases "on the house"? Is there a way for customers to feel like they're making progress toward their goal without actually doing anything?

PART FOUR
INDIVIDUAL

DOES YOUR EXPERIENCE USE RELEVANT DATA TO PERSONALIZE?

"People do not buy goods and services. They buy relations, stories and magic."

- Seth Godin, author and entrepreneur

What is an "individual" experience?

An "individual" experience feels like it was created for one person, rather than a group of name-less, face-less "customers". Brands like Amazon, Uber, and Netflix have raised the bar for a personalized customer experience. Fair or not, customer expectations for every company have been set by an innovative few. In order to keep up with these data-led brands, we first need to understand why personalization is so effective and how best to apply it.

NINE

INDIVIDUAL: THE COCKTAIL PARTY EFFECT

PEOPLE ARE MORE LIKELY TO RESPOND TO PERSONALIZED EXPERIENCES

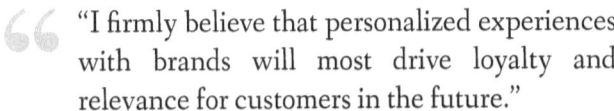

"I firmly believe that personalized experiences with brands will most drive loyalty and relevance for customers in the future."

— Katrina Lake, CEO of Stitch Fix

It seems like every company is chasing personalization. In fact, almost 70% of brands surveyed in an Everstring report[1] called it a "top priority." It could be easy to write personalization off as a shiny object, if not for the financial returns. In their 2019 "Personalization Development Study"[2], consultancy Monetate outlined the return on investment (ROI) of personalized marketing:

- **Personalized marketing drives growth**. 93% of companies with an "advanced personalization strategy" saw revenue growth. Only 45.4% of companies without a personalization strategy saw equivalent growth.
- **The higher the investment, the better**

the returns. Companies with ROI of 200% or more said personalization made up at least 20% of their marketing budget.

- **Personalization drives long-term customer value**. Brands that had the highest personalization ROI focused on loyalty as their top KPI. Companies with lower ROI targeted short term measures like average order value.

It's clear there's evidence supporting personalization. It compels customers to act, and they're actively asking for more. In a recent study[3], consulting firm Infosys found that 31% of customers wish their experiences were "far more" personalized. But why? The answer lies in a psychological principle known as the cocktail party effect.

This effect was discovered in the 1950s by a British cognitive scientist named Colin Cherry[4]. He wanted to understand what people focus on and why. After researching the dynamics of a noisy room, he discovered something interesting. Our brain separates overlapping conversations into different auditory streams. It can then decide to ignore information that isn't relevant.

The cocktail party effect states that people focus on information relevant to them. According to a study published in the journal *Brain Research*, a key trigger for "tuning in" is when people hear their name[5]. Given the research, it makes sense that brands start personalization efforts with a customer's name. But the cocktail party effect shows if we go deeper, relevant content can drive incredible results.

But personalization isn't just about getting your customer's first name right then spamming them with impersonal ads. As author and marketer Seth Godin said:

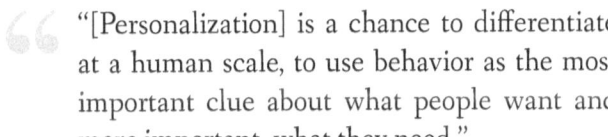 "[Personalization] is a chance to differentiate at a human scale, to use behavior as the most important clue about what people want and more important, what they need."

True personalization is deeply understanding your user's journey. Once you know what they need, you can serve them the right message at the right time, and drive results. There are three guiding principles of personalization to which all experiences need to adhere:

1. Get specific about your customer's world

In a recent study, Accenture discovered[6] three personalization tactics that have a direct effect on customer purchase decisions. Customers said:

- **Know my name**: 56% of customers would rather buy from a retailer that recognizes them by name.
- **Know my past**: 65% of customers prefer to buy from a retailer who "knows their purchase history."
- **Know what I want**: 58% of customers prefer to buy from a retailer that recommends options based on their past purchases.

An example of a brand that applies personalization well is the jewelry store Monica Vinader. By using customer data in a smart but subtle way, they create an appealing experience. For example, the brand sends out email marketing that features customized jewelry with the customer's first initial in their images. Because my first name is Jennifer, I would get an email with a "J" engraved on the featured product, while someone named Kim would get an image engraved with the initial "K." Not only that, but the type of product shown could be based on my previous purchases. So if I prefer to wear necklaces but bracelets are more Kim's style, those are the products we'll see in our respective emails.

2. Personalize your marketing's visuals, copy, and message

In their 2018 "Ecommerce Quarterly Report", Monetate discovered some interesting data regarding experience design and personalization[7]. For example:

- Just three pages of personalized content can potentially double conversion rates.
- The value of personalization compounds with each experience. In other words, if a user has a personalized experience three times, every time they engage, the experience becomes more persuasive.
- In a personalized experience, users add items to their cart more often, and cart abandonment rates decrease significantly.

The use of personalized marketing goes beyond just digital experiences. If, for instance, you're designing a retail experience consider how broader segmentation can help reach customers when one-on-one personalization may not be possible. For example, you could:

- **Feature the name or skyline of a**

store's location. Starbucks does this to great effect by localizing its shops with mugs, murals, and references to the local state or city.

- **Can you segment your stores based on demographic and purchase data to understand who's shopping there the most?** For instance, a Target near a suburban neighborhood might stock more healthy grocery items for families. A store in a college town, on the other hand, might create an experience tailored for students by stocking more clothes, snacks, and alcohol.

3. Go deeper with data — and be transparent

Your ability to personalize effectively is directly tied to the state of your brand's data. And if the data is there but it isn't in shape, getting to the right insights might mean digging a little deeper. Further research could take the form of progressive profiling (sending out a survey to get to know your customers better), marketing automation, or just asking your customers if the marketing they're getting is right for them.

British airline EasyJet made a company milestone relevant to its customers by using data. Instead of making their 20th anniversary about the brand, EasyJet focused on the consumer. They transformed people's data into an email that celebrated their travels with EasyJet, by listing every trip the customer had taken with them in the last twenty years. EasyJet also told customers where the data had originated, so the communication was transparent, not creepy.

The bottom line

Personalization is a top priority for brands, but most haven't achieved their ambitions. And that's a problem because the stakes are high. According to a recent survey by research firm Gardner, 38% of customers said they would abandon a company after receiving poor personalization[8].

There's no magic button you can press to make your experience personalized. It's a tough process that requires experience teams to work closely with IT, marketing operations, and digital teams. But at the end of the day, the potential for revenue generation is huge. The science supports it, and customers are asking for it.

TO APPLY the cocktail party effect, ask yourself:

- Are there moments in our experience where we can put our data to work for the customer? If we use data to personalize the experience, are we making the value exchange clear?
- Beyond any legal implications for requesting or using customer data, are we being *too personalized?* In other words, are we creeping people out? Make sure to manage your customers' emotions in the experience as much as the amount of personalization. The appropriate level of customization may be different for different types of customers as well, so make sure you're clear when you ask customers how they'd like their data used.
- Using algorithms to know and predict your customers has powerful implications for the

ability to personalize. For example, suggestive selling algorithms are an excellent opportunity to use personalization, as well as trending products. "Next best item" algorithms can even help customers complete an outfit based on a single item in their cart, or remember something they may have otherwise forgotten to buy (batteries, for instance).

- When we personalize our experience and communications, are we going "beyond the name"? Remember, true personalization is the opportunity to "differentiate at scale" as Seth Godin put it. It can prove to be a unique selling proposition if put to good use.

———

TEN

INDIVIDUAL: THE SELF-REFERENCE EFFECT

PEOPLE WILL ENGAGE MORE WHEN INFORMATION IS RELEVANT TO THEM

 "You don't create new worlds to give them all the same limits of the old ones."

— Jane Espenson, author

Have you ever spent an entire video call looking at yourself on screen? Nothing's more fascinating to people than themselves. In fact, people spend 60% of a conversation talking about themselves[1]. When people use social media, this[2] jumps to 80%. People's brains even code information differently when it's about them. Why? It's down to a behavioral science principle known as the self-reference effect.

This effect states that people remember information more easily when it's relevant to them[3]. Our brains encode personalized information differently, resulting in enhanced recall, learning, and persuasion[4]. Several studies have found that customers are more likely to respond to ads when the models look like them[5]. Referencing a customer's *internal picture* of themselves is even more powerful. For example, if a woman thinks of herself as "strong", she's more likely to prefer experiences that reference "strength". If she's shopping for running gear and notices the female mannequins have obvious muscle tone, she'll see the experience as more relevant to her.

There are many ways to apply the self-reference effect to a customer experience. Three brands that do it well include:

1. Dove soap: Reflect your customers in your advertising

In the early 2000s, the Dove personal care brand discovered its customers didn't see themselves reflected in beauty marketing. Featured models were nearly all tall, thin, white, and young. This visual uniformity had a negative impact on how women felt about their looks. In fact, Dove found that "only 4% of women[6] around the world consider themselves beautiful." This insight, and others like it, drove Dove to create the Real Beauty campaign.

The brand began championing female empowerment by using more diverse models, and the results were incredible. In the first ten years of the campaign, sales jumped from $2.5 to $4 billion[7]. Dove bars became the number one preferred soap brand in the U.S., and the product became parent company Unilever's best selling product.

2. Optimizely: Create a hyper-relevant experience

Optimizely works with big brands to perfect their digital content. But the company's biggest challenge is making sure the leads gathered from their own contact forms are strong. As Takeshi Young, the Digital Marketing Manager at Optimizely wrote[8]:

> "Although many visitors would create accounts, lots of them were unqualified, with incomplete lead data. This created problems further down the sales funnel..."

To meet this challenge, Optimizely created 26 different versions of their website. Different audiences would see a different landing page. For example, unknown customers would see a different page from customers who'd spent a few hours reading the Optimizely blog. They even created specific landing pages with cu for potential customers, like Adidas and Microsoft.

After implementing this self-reference strategy, Optimizely saw impressive results:

- 113% increase in conversions to their "solutions" page
- 117% increase in conversions to the account creation process

3. Brooks Footwear: Use dynamic digital content

The self-reference effect can also be used to reflect a customer's environment. In fact, 60% of marketers[9] say using contextual signals such as location, weather, and temperature, drives action. Brooks, a running shoe brand, used this insight to create dynamic emails based on a user's environment. If their local weather was warm and sunny, customers would get an email featuring a runner wearing shorts with the headline, "Hot weather, cool runs". If the weather was rainy and cold, they'd see a headline image of a woman wearing a jacket with the headline, "Don't take a rain check on your run".

The bottom line

The self-reference effect can be a powerful tool when designing customer experiences. Reflecting your customers' personal identities can drive engagement, brand love, and sales.

TO APPLY THE SELF-REFERENCE EFFECT, ask yourself:

- **How deeply do we know our customers?** Not just their demographic information, but their thoughts, fear, goals, and aspirations? Does our experience reflect how they see themselves?
- **Are we creating experiences that reflect the customer's environment?** For example, are people getting ads for winter coats when it's 80 degrees outside? If it's cold outside, are we trying to sell them ice cream? Is there something unique about where they live and work that we need to take into consideration when designing their experience?

—

PART FIVE

CONTEXTUAL

DOES THE CONTEXT OF YOUR EXPERIENCE SUBTLY GUIDE CUSTOMER CHOICE?

"People spend money when and where they feel good."

– Walt Disney, founder of the Walt Disney Company

What is a "contextual" experience?

The context of a choice is critical when persuading customers to take action. It consists of two elements:

1. The **mechanics** of a choice
2. The **environment** surrounding a choice, also called the choice architecture

For example, designing a "contextual" purchase experience for a software product would involve structuring both the choice mechanics and the environment.

The **mechanics** of the decision might include how we charge customers—for instance, creating a monthly subscription that's automatically charged to a credit card, rather than forcing customers to login and pay every month.
The **environmental** context might include how we present the information surrounding a choice. For instance, we might add a "secret agent" product that makes another option look more attractive in comparison. We might also expose customers to a large number before we show the prices of our products. This large number would make our prices seem like a good value in comparison. Both the mechanical and environmental context of a choice architecture can make a significant impact on what decision a customer will make.

—

ELEVEN

CONTEXTUAL: DEFAULTS

MOST PEOPLE WON'T DEVIATE FROM THE PRE-SET OPTION

 "... Never underestimate the power of inertia.

— Richard H. Thaler, economist and Nobel laureate

Are you enrolled in a retirement plan, 401k, or pension? If your answer is no, you might want to check again. Your company may have registered you automatically because they knew you weren't likely to do it on your own. In fact, automatic enrollment increases participation in retirement plans by nearly 40%[1]. Why? It's down to a psychological principle known as default bias.

Defaults are pre-set choices that take effect if a person does nothing. A common example would be the default settings on an account or website. Studies have shown[2] that people rarely change default settings, and Microsoft found that 95% of people kept all defaults[3]. That number was consistent even for critical features, like autosave. Default bias describes our tendency to favor these pre-set choices.

The most cited example of the impact of defaults is in the area of organ donation rates[4]. In countries where citizens are automatically opted-in to an organ donation program, most people are organ donors. But in those countries where people are asked to opt-in to organ donation, fewer people join. For example, in France, an opt-out country, 99.98% of people are organ donors. In Germany, where people must actively opt-in to donate, only 12% of citizens are organ donors[5].

Why do defaults work?

When it comes to thinking, people are lazy[6]. Defaults provide a mental shortcut. They also signal what we're "supposed" to do in a given situation. Since defaults don't require people to make any effort, they can be a simple but powerful experience design tool. For example, Amazon's default purchase option is "Subscribe & Save". It's always pre-selected in the checkout area. If the user does nothing they might get a monthly subscription for paper towels instead of one shipment. The nice thing about this effect, for Amazon, is that most people don't take the time to notice and change this default option, resulting in accidental recurring revenue.

Although the concept of defaults is easy to grasp, applying them can be more complicated. According to researchers Daniel G. Goldstein, Eric J. Johnson, Andreas Herrmann, and Mark Heitmann, there are six types of defaults. Their article, "Nudge Your Customers Toward Better Choices", published in Harvard Business Review, outlines how brands commonly use these principles.

1. Mass defaults

Mass defaults apply to all people, without customizing for individual features or preferences. A common example would be an online checkout process that auto-selects "2-day shipping" for every customer. This might be a more expensive option for the customer, but it's pre-selected because the company knows most people won't change it.

2. Benign defaults

Benign defaults are a brand's best guess about what a customer wants. The authors give an example[7] of benign default options for child's carseats:

 "The shoulder straps on Maxi-Cosi car seats can be threaded through either of two sets of holes, a lower set for newborns or a higher one for older children.

Which setting should be the default?

Using the higher strap setting could endanger a newborn, as the straps won't hold her securely. Yet the lower one would be uncomfortable for an older child. Here the benign default is obvious. Most customers purchase this type of car seat for newborns."

3. Hidden options

In this case, the default is presented as the only choice, even though there are alternatives. These "hidden options" are available, but often hard to find. This type of default is often used in software development.

Designers don't want to confuse casual users with too many options, or with options that have the potential to break the experience. So instead, they put the "hidden options" in a spot that's difficult to find. That way, an advanced user can change defaults, but only if they're willing to search for them.

4. Smart defaults

These defaults are based on customer data, either at a personal level or as a part of a customer segment. Often these are designed with geographic or demographic information. For example, if you've filled out a profile for an investment site, and the system knows you're a 22-year-old who makes $19,000 a year, they'll present a different set of default options than a 55-year-old partner in a law firm.

5. Persistent defaults

These use a customer's past choices to dictate their future defaults. For example, if you always choose a window seat on an airplane, an airline might automatically assign you a window seat. These defaults have the potential to surprise and delight customers or creep them out. If you want to employ persistent defaults based on customer data, it helps to be transparent about where the data came from.

A simple note at the bottom of an email can help turn a persistent default into a great experience. For example, including a message such as, "We've automatically given you a window seat because our records say you've booked a window seat for 85% of your recorded trips with Delta Airlines. Is this still your preference?"

6. Adaptive defaults

Adaptive defaults update themselves in real-time, acting as advisors to help people find a perfect set of features. For example, when shopping for a car online, users could be asked if they'd like a sports, comfort, or economy vehicle. As the customer makes their choices, options change based on the information they're sharing in real-time.

How defaults can change the meaning of a choice

In a 2012 study, researchers found that the presence of a default can change what we think of a person who opts out[8]. For example, consider someone whose state has an opt-in organ donation policy. This person then chooses *not* to become an organ donor. In this situation, observers perceived the non-donor to be an immoral person. Under an opt-out policy, people who asked to be removed from the donor program were perceived as having even worse morals than those who didn't opt-in. The research team saw this social pressure affecting people's behavior in real-time. In the study, when subjects were watched by other people while making their choice, they were more likely to become an organ donor[9].

The bottom line

The default effect is one of the most powerful principles in behavioral science. We have to be thoughtful about what default choices we include, and sometimes the best default for the company is not the best thing for the customer. Set the default options to the path you want users to take, but consider the implications of this path. Most customers won't hunt for hidden options, read the owner's manual, or make considered choices.

As Charles Arthur wrote in his article "Why the default settings on your device should be right the first time"[10]:

 "95% of users don't change a damn thing...if you think that most people are going to voluntarily download and install a different web browser for their new phone, or download a different app to do email from the one that came on their computer, you're dreaming."

TO APPLY DEFAULTS, ask yourself:

- What is the optimal journey we want customers to take? Are there any "forks in the road" where we can create a default that helps our customers?
- When we consider our business objectives for this exeprience, are there any moments we feel customers feel confused and might benefit from "hidden options"?
- Are there opportunities to better use our customer data to reduce friction in their journey, by predicting what they might want or need and making that their default experience?
- Identify where we're making a decision for our customers by including a default. Does the

customer still feel empowered at these decision points? Or do they feel trapped by the default, or like they're being encouraged to make an unhealthy choice?

TWELVE

CONTEXTUAL: THE CASHLESS EFFECT

PEOPLE WILL SPEND MORE WHEN THEY CAN AVOID THE "PAIN OF PAYMENT"

"There is only one boss. The customer—and he can fire everybody in the company from the chairman on down, simply by spending his money somewhere else."

—Sam Walton, founder of Walmart

Have you ever heard of the envelope budgeting method? It's a simple system that relies on people putting cash into separate envelopes for different parts of their budget like groceries and the rent. It can be useful for those who feel their money seems to "slip away" during the month on small purchases. But there's also a psychological reason why using cash makes it easier to stick to a budget. It's down to a principle called the cashless effect.

This effect[1] states that the more tangible payments are, the more psychologically painful it is for customers to spend money. We call this the "pain of payment". It's why people on a budget find it easier to track their spending when they use cash instead of credit cards. The more painful it feels to pay, the less money people will spend.

The cashless effect has been studied in many different scenarios. For example, in one study, researchers found[2] that people spent more when apartment laundry rooms took cards instead of coins. In another study, researchers at the Massachuttses Institute of Technology (MIT)[3] asked people to bid for a pair of tickets to a sporting event. One group was told they'd be paying with a credit card, and the other group was told they'd be paying with cash. The subjects in the credit card group bid up to 72% more for the tickets than those who were told they'd be paying with cash.

The cashless effect can be applied in a variety of customer experiences, and brands love it because it's an easy way to remove friction from the purchase process. Let's look at a few brands that have found value in applying the cashless effect.

1. Panera Bread: MyPanera+Coffee

Panera, the bakery-café chain, introduced an unlimited coffee subscription in 2020. Called MyPanera+Coffee, the program offers unlimited hot coffee, iced coffee, and tea at all Panera restaurants for $8.99 a month. Customers can get free refills in-store every two hours. When customers add a coffee subscription to their MyPanera rewards account, they pay the fee automatically each month by credit card. By adding +Coffee to the rewards redemption process, Panera removed the "pain of payment" when buying a coffee. The experience of scanning an app for a pre-paid cup of coffee is so painless, it almost feels like getting something for nothing.

Before rolling MyPanera+Coffee out to all cafes, the company tested the program in 150 stores for three months. Although many were skeptical of the pilot, the bottom-line results speak for themselves:

- **The frequency of visits jumped by more than 200%** for customers who signed up for MyPanera+Coffee[4].
- **There was a 70% increase in food attachment for subscribers**, which Panera CEO Niren Chaudhary called "staggering." In other words, people who came in to get their subscription coffee also bought food. Before using the program, they were more likely to come in and only buy a cup of coffee[5].

2. Amazon: 1-Click Ordering

Amazon is the Terminator of eCommerce — it's ever-evolving, learning, and growing. Because so many people shop at Amazon, it's able to test on a massive scale which gives them the benefit of learning on a massive scale as well. So it's no surprise that when it comes to eliminating the pain of payment from their experience, Amazon is ahead of the curve.

The cashless effect is apparent in many parts of Amazon's experience, but 1-Click ordering is the primary example. Described by the company as a system that "places your order automatically and lets you skip the shopping basket." The first time you place an order, 1-Click ordering is automatically enabled. Any following order you make will be charged to your default payment method and delivered to your default address.

The bottom line

Using cash is a huge source of friction in any experience, as demonstrated by the cashless effect. But by eliminating the customer's pain of payment, you can create an experience that is not only pleasurable, but profitable as well.

TO APPLY THE CASHLESS EFFECT, ask yourself:

- How much friction, or difficulty, is there for customers in our payment process now?
- How many times do we ask them to pay? Are there any opportunities to provide a subscription option?
- How does our experience encourage the use of credit cards, prepaid cards, or virtual credits? Is there a way for us to incentivize their use that's both good for us and good for the customer?
- Are there ways for us to eliminate the pain of payment and improve our overall experience for customers as well?

THIRTEEN

CONTEXTUAL: THE ANCHORING EFFECT

PEOPLE ARE UNCONSCIOUSLY INFLUENCED BY THE FIRST INFORMATION THEY SEE

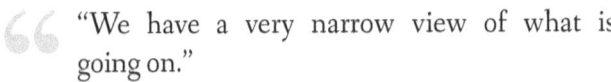 "We have a very narrow view of what is going on."

— Daniel Kahneman

Have you ever bought something just because it was on sale? Your rational mind knows that the sale price is never the real price. But you were persuaded by the deal. "It's 50% off," you said to yourself, "I've saved so much money!".

Seeing the regular price and then the sale price influenced you. It made you feel like you were getting an unmissable deal. But in reality, the business will still make money off the reduced price. And holding a sale triggered a purchase that they wouldn't have gotten otherwise. So why are sales such a powerful persuasion tool? It's all down to a behavioral science principle known as the anchoring effect.

Discovered by researchers Tversky and Kahneman, the anchoring effect states that decisions are influenced by the first information we see. We anchor to this information without being consciously aware of its effects[1]. This principle has been rigorously researched, in situations as varied as house prices, legal judgments, and purchasing decisions[23].

In 2006, researcher Dan Ariely led an experiment at MIT. He held an auction with a twist. He showed students in his class random objects, like a bottle of wine or a textbook. Ariely then asked students to write down a fake price for the item using the last two digits of their Social Security number as if it was the price. So for example, if my Social Security number was 123–45–6789, the price of a bottle of wine would be $89.

After students wrote down the fake price of each item, they bid on it in an auction. The results? Students who had high Social Security numbers paid up to 346% more than those with low numbers, for the same items. Why? Because the first number students saw — even though it was completely unrelated — unconsciously influenced how much they decided to bid. The higher the Social Security number, the higher the bid.

As Dan Ariely put it in his book "Predictably Irrational":

 "Social security numbers were the anchor in this experiment only because we requested them.

We could have just as well asked for the current temperature or the manufacturer's suggested retail price.

Any question, in fact, would have created the anchor. Does that seem rational? Of course not."

Many brands apply the anchoring effect without realizing it. For example:

1. Amazon

Amazon is often guilty of showing a high normal price, also called the "list price", to anchor customers. The New York Times article "Some Online Bargains May Only Look Like One", describes the strategy this way[4]:

> "List price is a largely fictitious concept, promoted by the brand... and adopted by the retailer to compel the customer into pushing the buy button."

One extreme example on Amazon was a cat litter box with a "list" price of $2,000. It's now being sold at the bargain price of $27.67. There's nothing special about this litter box, it's not made out of gold. It's just a run of the mill plastic cat box that's 99.99% off.

Customers anchor to the list price, and in comparison, it looks like they're getting a fantastic deal. And as we know from Ariely's Social Security example, an unrelated number will still influence later decisions. It doesn't matter that the list price is outrageously high. It just matters that customers see it and it gets them to buy.

2. Walgreens

Multiple-unit pricing is a common psychological strategy. It's best described as offering a "Get 10 for $5", or similar offer. If you're in the United States, and you pick up any

Walgreens or CVS weekly ad, you'll see the anchoring effect in action.

In their paper, "Multiple unit price promotions and their effects on quantity purchase intentions," researchers Kenneth Manning and David Sprott explain that people are more likely to buy if the quantity of purchase is higher[5]. In other words, a 10 for $10 deal is more convincing than a 5 for $5. Why? Because customers anchor on the first number they see, they begin to rationalize why they need ten bottles of dish soap instead of one. They might only buy five, but that's four more than they intended to buy when they came into the store.

The anchoring effect can be applied in several different ways, but it's commonly used when pricing products. To apply the effect, try to:

1. Add premium-priced anchor products

Feature a premium product with a much higher price point than the rest of your catalog. This product's job isn't to sell, but to make everything else seem like a good deal. J.Crew uses this strategy on their website. High-priced "anchor products", much higher priced than the average customer would expect to see in a J.Crew store, are merchandised next to "normal-priced" products.

For example, a random merchandising of three JCrew.com coats includes a $1500 anchor-priced coat next to two similar styled coats priced at $99. This anchor product is intended to do two things: make the $99 puffer coats look like a steal in comparison and create a halo of prestige around the cheaper items. The customer thinks, "If this brand is prestigious enough to charge $1500 for a coat, I'm still getting a nice quality coat for $99 but without the high price tag. Plus, I'll get the prestige of wearing a brand that sells $1500 coats."

2. Add high initial anchor prices

By showing customers the "normal" price and the sale price, you give them something to anchor against when deciding if they're getting a deal. This strategy does carry some risk, however. As in the earlier Amazon example, if you set the "anchor price" too high, you risk treading in an ethical grey area. You also run the risk of training customers to only buy when there are steep discounts, which can damage your brand in the long-term[6].

The bottom line

The anchoring effect means we need to be mindful of what we show customers, especially in the early stages of digital experiences. Weigh the pros and cons of tinkering with the anchoring effect. It can be a tricky, but very effective, behavioral science effect with which to experiment.

TO APPLY THE ANCHORING EFFECT, ask yourself:

- Is it possible that we're anchoring our customers to a number somewhere early in our experience? Could we do more to position our highest-priced products first, in order to make our core products seem like more of a bargain?
- Is any anchoring in our experience reflective of our brand? For instance, anchoring needs to do a different job for a luxury brand than for a

chain of fast-food restaurants. Not everyone is looking for a bargain, and people use price to gauge value.

- Could we insert an anchoring moment into our physical or digital experience? Is it possible that we're missing an opportunity to use strategic pricing to our advantage?

FOURTEEN

CONTEXTUAL: SOCIAL PROOF

PEOPLE ARE MORE LIKELY TO TAKE ACTION IF IT SEEMS LIKE A SOCIAL NORM

> "Men, it has been well said, think in herds; it will be seen that they go mad in herds, while they only recover their senses slowly, one by one."

— Charles MacKay, author and journalist

In any user or customer experience, we ask people to make a lot of decisions. Often these decisions are low risk, like which color sweatshirt to buy or how much memory a new phone needs. For options that don't carry too much risk, it's easy to guide customer choices. A simple tactic like prompting with a default can be impactful[1]. But what about decisions that are a little bit riskier?

When asked to make novel or high stakes choices, like buying a new car, customers feel anxious and unsure.[2] Decisions like these call for a strong persuasion tactic - a psychological principle known as social proof.

Coined by Stanford professor Robert Cialdini, social proof describes the human tendency to look at what other people are doing to gain psychological permission to try something new[3]. According to research, 83% of consumers in 60 countries say they trust social proof more than any other form of persuasion[4]. This principle can be applied to an experience in several ways:

1. Define social norms and ask users to follow them

People like to adhere to social norms, especially when they know or relate to the group[5]. Describe desired behaviors as common and valued in the community. Make people feel like "everyone's doing it, except you." For example, social norms messaging has been shown to increase sales of healthy food[6]. When people in a cafeteria saw a sign that read, "every day over 50 of our customers buy a salad", more of them chose a healthy side option.

2. Make it easy for customers to see what other people think of your experience

One of the most effective ways to apply social proof is through product reviews and testimonials. According to Mintel research, more than 70% of Americans ask other people for opinions before making a purchase[7]. The younger the consumer, the more likely they are to seek out the opinions of others - 81% percent of 18 to 34 year-olds look for reviews and testimonials before buying a product.

3. Get an expert to recommend your product

People have to risk a bad experience to try something new. But when an authority on the subject suggest a product or service, customers are more likely to believe it will work[8]. Expert recommendations build trust and reduce the risk associated with trying your product.

4. Use numbers to deliver social proof

Communicating how many people already use your product or service helps reduce perceived risk. For example, Hubspot relies on numbers to get more users to join their mailing list. In a pop-up message on their website, they ask people to "join 215,000 fellow marketers" already subscribed to the Hubspot newsletter. By referencing the size of their email list, Hubspot appeals to people's reliance on crowds to decide if its product is worth the risk.

The bottom line

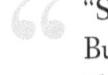 "Social proof can be delivered in many ways. But its effectiveness generally stems from the idea that we, as humans, find safety and comfort in pursuing the unknown if we know that others have done the same and found success."

— Dennis Pavlina, manager at Widerfunnel

Research has shown that social proof is the most effective customer persuasion tactic[9]. The best part? It's relatively easy and cheap to implement. You just have to reframe product and service messages using social proof.

· · ·

TO APPLY SOCIAL PROOF, ask yourself:

- Where are the risky moments in our experience? How can we include a social proof message to mitigate this risk?
- Are there certain products that people might be willing to try if the risk were lower? Perhaps one that's high margin for your business but is only around for a limited time. How can you normalize the use of this new product?
- Can data help us tell a persuasive story about risk? For example, the Body Shop sends out a samples of their Hemp Hard-Working Hand Protection balm that stated a tube was "sold every nine seconds". A brilliant way to help customers consider a new product.

FIFTEEN

CONTEXTUAL: LOSS AVERSION

PEOPLE FEAR LOSS 2X MORE THAN THEY ENJOY WINNING

 "Is everyone hanging out without me?"

— Mindy Kaling, author and actor

Have you ever experienced FOMO, or the "fear of missing out"? It's a form of social anxiety that makes people scared they're being left out of exciting or interesting events[1]. It's usually triggered by posts on social media, where it looks like the whole world is having fun without you.

If you suffer from FOMO, you're not alone. An Eventbrite study found that 70% of millennials experience the fear of missing out regularly[2]. There's a profound psychological principle behind why people experience FOMO. It's called loss aversion, and it can be a powerful design tool for guiding customer choice.

First identified by Nobel laureate Daniel Kahneman, loss aversion is a psychological principle that says people will go to great lengths to avoid losing[3]. In fact, the psychological pain of losing is twice as powerful as the pleasure of winning[4]. Because it's so powerful, loss aversion features heavily in cognitive psychology and decision theory. It's also one of the most effective tactics for getting customers to buy, the other being social proof[5]. A customer's fear of losing can take lots of forms, each with fascinating applications:

1. How information is presented can dramatically impact decision-making

A study was conducted to see if framing cancer treatments using loss aversion could improve surgery opt-in rates[6]. The research team hypothesized that opt-in rates were related to how the options were framed. To test this hypothesis, doctors presented patients with two options. Each option framed surgery as either a potential gain or a possible loss, and the results were staggering.

When surgery was framed as a gain with the message, "the one-month survival rate of surgery is 90%", 84% of people chose surgery. But when the surgery was framed as a loss with the message, "there is a 10% chance of death in the month post-surgery", only 50% of people opted for surgery. The use of loss aversion to frame surgery as a gain increased opt-ins by 54%.

2. Ownership creates emotional bonds that people don't want to break

This principle is known as the endowment effect. It's a psychological principle that falls under the loss aversion umbrella. In his book, "Predictably Irrational," Dan Ariely describes this effect through the lens of Duke University basketball. If you're unfamiliar with Duke basketball, all you need to know is the Duke versus the University of North Carolina game is the biggest of the year. It takes place in an area of the country where basketball is a religion. To score tickets to this game, students have to camp out for weeks. They then enter a lottery for a chance to win tickets.

Ariely reached out to students who won tickets and those who entered the lottery but didn't win. Both had invested the same amount of pain, sacrifice, time, and effort to enter the lottery. But some had won, and others hadn't. Would this affect how each group valued the basketball tickets? Students who were not successful in the lottery said they'd pay an average of $170 for a ticket. But the students who did get a ticket? When asked how much they'd sell their ticket for, they asked 170% more, about $2,400 on average. Why were the ticket owners asking for so much more money?Emotion. According to Ariely, once someone owns a product, they begin fantasizing about their future experiences. Once they create these "pre-memories" of the game, ticket-holders don't want to lose out. So these students wouldn't only be selling a ticket. They'd be losing out on potential memories, emotions, and good times.

The lesson? The more emotions associated with a product, the more people value it. So how can we apply loss aversion to our experience?

1. Create FOMO with "only a few left" messaging:

Travel and hotel sites, such as Booking.com, often use loss aversion to nudge sales. When customers are browsing hotel deals, they see a loss aversion message such as "Only 6 rooms left!" This copy pushes customers who might be on the fence to buy before they miss out.

It is worth noting that in the U.K., several brands stopped using this language because the numbers they displayed were not based in fact, but were randomly generated. Clearly making up fake numbers to drive a false sense of scarcity is not ethical. However, if the numbers are correct and reflect real-time inventory, there's nothing inherently wrong with informing your customers.

2. Create a sense of impending loss with a countdown clock

Any launch, limited time offer, or sale can benefit from including a countdown clock. You don't have to use a literal clock, however. Digital channels paired with re-marketing are a great way to apply loss aversion. You can send an email or display an ad to remind customers that there's limited stock of an item they put in their basket but didn't buy. Both of these options create a sense of urgency, and customers begin to fear that if they miss out on this opportunity, it may not be back for a while.

Be aware that you will set customer expectations, the more you use a countdown clock or imply that this deal or offer won't happen again. If your brand comes back with a better sale two weeks later, customers will notice, and you'll begin to erode their trust. You'll also train them to wait for sales and promo codes before buying.

3. Create an emotional bond with free trials

If you want to produce the endowment effect, like Professor Ariely, a free product trial is effective. Once your product is in a customer's home, an emotional bond is developed through use. The feeling of ownership is a powerful psychological tool for getting and keeping customers.

The bottom line

The danger of using traditional loss aversion signals is that they can come across as spammy. Phrases like "last chance!" and "hurry up!" can turn some people off, or get an email sent directly to the spam folder[7]. People are smart, and they don't want to feel like you're manipulating them. So how do you use loss aversion without sounding spammy? It's simple — have empathy for your customers. Dive deeper to truly get to know their pains and fears. Only use loss aversion in situations where risk actually exists, and always be transparent and truthful.

TO APPLY LOSS AVERSION, ask yourself:

- Do you understand specifically what your audience is afraid of losing? Why are they scared of losing this service, product, or knowledge?
- Do you touchpoints address our customer's worries and issues? More importantly, does our experience provide a potential solution that's framed as a way to avoid loss?
- Do you know your customer's hopes, goals, and fears better than your competitors?
- If your brand is in the luxury or fashion space, you can still use loss aversion to your advantage. Many of these products exist because they

signal "achievement" and "luxury" to other people. They are status symbols as much as products. Ask yourself what your customers stand to lose if they couldn't use your products as symbols.

SIXTEEN

CONTEXTUAL: THE DECOY EFFECT

PEOPLE MAKE CHOICES BY COMPARING THE OPTIONS IN FRONT OF THEM

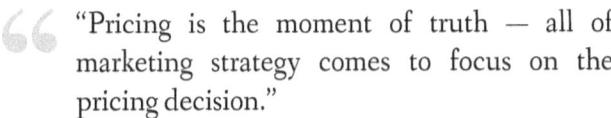 "Pricing is the moment of truth — all of marketing strategy comes to focus on the pricing decision."

— Prof. E. Raymond Corey, Harvard Business School

Every experience needs to drive sales. But not all sales are created equal. Some are more profitable than others. In any given product line, items that seem like they'd provide similar profitability, often don't. That's because the cost to market, manage, and sell a product doesn't have a direct correlation with the final price. Products that cost less to sell bring in a bigger percentage of their sale price — they're more profitable. So how do you get customers to pick the option that's best for your bottom line?

There are a few tactics you could use to get customers to choose the right product. For example you could:

1. Decrease the total number of choices to make your experience simpler.
2. Keep your high-margin products top of mind with the mere exposure effect.
3. Reduce the risk of trying a new, high-margin product by using social proof.

But there's a way to price your products that will make the high-margin product an easy choice for customers. It takes advantage of a proven psychological trigger. It's called the decoy effect, and it's a research-backed way to influence customer choice.

The decoy effect describes how price comparisons between products affect choice. It states that when there are only two options, and they're priced fairly, people make decisions according to personal preference. But, if there's a third choice that's overpriced compared to the first two options, it changes how people consider all of their choices. The third option is a "decoy" choice. The decoy's purpose is to change perceptions of the other options, not sell. Why? Because customers compare the other products against the decoy. And because the decoy price is unreasonably high, everything else seems reasonable in comparison.

The decoy effect works because people don't know what an item should cost in isolation. People use comparison to other options to determine the relative price, and therefore value, of an item. Without anything to compare an item with, customers tend to make do with guesses.

Examples of the decoy effect in action

The best way to demonstrate the decoy effect is to work through some real life examples. Below you'll find two choice sets — one without a decoy , and one with a decoy.

An example of a choice set with no decoy could be two cars:

- Used 1972 Volkswagon Beatle with a price tag of $10,000
- New 2021 Porche Cayenne with a price tag of $60,000

In this example, the options are far apart both in features and in price. A customer looking at these two options would be swayed more by their own needs than the car's price. If, for instance, a potential buyer is a 70-year-old woman who needs to drive less than 5 miles a week, and only needs enough room for her and her groceries, the VW is the obvious choice. An upper middle-class family of four, however, would be a better fit for the Porsche.

A common example of a choice set that includes a decoy option would be coffee cup sizes. For instance:

- A small coffee costs $2.00
- A medium coffee is $6.50
- A large coffee costs $7.00

In the example above, the price of the medium coffee ($6.50) acts as the decoy opion to push more people toward a large ($7.00). The price difference between the small ($2.00) and the medium ($6.50) is much more than the price difference between the medium and the large. The greater the difference between the decoy and the low-priced option, the greater the decoy effect.

This principle uses price differences to change a customer's perceptions and resulting behavior. Dan Ariely described the effect this way, in his book *Predictably Irrational*[1]:

> "The decoy effect is the phenomenon whereby consumers will tend to have a specific change in preference between two options when also presented with a third option that is asymmetrically dominated.
>
> This effect is the 'secret agent' in many decisions."

Ariely proved the efficacy of this "secret agent" with a study on subscription options[2]. He asked people to choose which version of the Economist they'd prefer to buy. In the "no decoy" experiment, there was only a digital version ($59) and a print version ($125). However, in the decoy experiment, there were three options:

1. A digital-only option ($59)
2. A print-only option ($125) — **the decoy option**
3. A combination package where customers got both digital and print versions for the same price as the print-only option ($125)

The print-only option was the decoy. It cost the same as the digital and print combination but was an inferior choice. In the no decoy experiment, 68% of customers bought the digital-only option, and 32% bought print-only. The total revenue was $8,012.

In the decoy experiment, no one bought the print only version - the decoy. 84% of customers purchased the print+digital combination, and 16% bought digital only. The total revenue was $11,444. The introduction of a decoy option immediately raised total revenue by over 42%.

The bottom line

The best way to test the decoy effect is to launch an experiment. You can use a small group of customers as a test, before launching it to the broader customer base. It's vital to understand how different customers with different needs will react to your decoy option before going wide. Points of decision are the best moments in customer and user journeys to apply the decoy effect. As Jeff Bezos said,

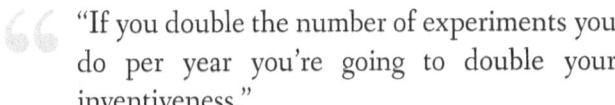

"If you double the number of experiments you do per year you're going to double your inventiveness."

TO APPLY THE DECOY EFFECT, ask yourself:

- If I examine my product mix, what's the "best" item I can sell? The "best" item might not be the highest-priced item, but rather one that's attractive for both your margin and the brand.
- How am I selling that product at the moment?

What other products are shown in a comparison set with this "best" item?

- On what dimensions would customers be comparing these products? Are the points of comparison clear, before considering the price?
- Now that you've designed a choice set and designated clear points of comparison, plan your first decoy. Follow the step-by-step process below to get started:

1. Choose the product you want to sell the most
2. Create three product choices
3. Make sure these three choices include a "secret agent" decoy option
4. Price the decoy close to the high-priced option
5. Make the decoy only marginally better than the low-priced option

PART SIX
EMOTIONAL

DO CUSTOMERS HAVE POSITIVE EMOTIONS AND MEMORIES ASSOCIATED WITH YOUR EXPERIENCE?

"The mind is no match with the heart in persuasion."

- Everett Dirksen, politician

What is an "emotional" experience?

People who design customer and user experiences often shy away from creating specific emotional states. We might feel that planning to create certain emotions is manipulative. Or we might think that emotions are too unpredictable to design. Regardless of our personal feelings, the science is clear on how important emotions are for users and customers. Therefore, when creating or managing an experience, we need to understand how people might interpret and remember it.

In this section, we'll discuss the science behind how

memories are created - good or bad - and what makes customers more likely to bond to an experience.

SEVENTEEN
EMOTIONAL: THE IKEA EFFECT
PEOPLE BECOME BONDED TO EXPERIENCES THEY HELP CREATE

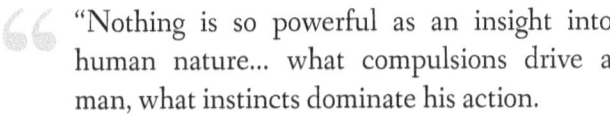 "Nothing is so powerful as an insight into human nature... what compulsions drive a man, what instincts dominate his action.

If you know these things about a man you can touch him at the core of his being."

— Bill Bernbach

In the 1950s, the Betty Crocker brand was in crisis. They needed to sell more of their instant cake mixes. The product seemed like a winner — just add water, and you'll have a delicious cake, ready to bake. But sales struggles led parent company General Mills to seek outside help. Ernest Dichter, the "father of motivational research," came in to assist.

Dichter discovered that a totally instant cake mix was too easy. Home bakers of the time felt it undervalued the skill of making a cake. "Remove the powdered egg," Dichter advised, "and have bakers add a fresh egg them-

selves. Give the baker more ownership of the final result."
Puzzled but desperate, General Mills reworked the recipe.

When adding an egg, bakers felt more involved in the process. They felt that they had contributed something deeper to the experience than just stirring together some water and a mix. Soon, sales of the semi-instant cake mix skyrocketed. All because Betty Crocker asked customers to become co-creators with the brand[1].

Co-creation means involving customers in the process of making or designing your experience[2]. Just like the Betty Crocker story, it can be as simple as asking customers to add an egg. Or as complex as asking them to assemble IKEA furniture. As long as customers know that the experience needs their input on a fundamental level, they're co-creating.

Co-creation can take many forms: assembling the finished product, coming up with new product ideas, solving problems, or even designing technical solutions. But why does co-creation work so well? It's down to a behavioral science principle known as the IKEA effect.

Coined by researchers at Harvard University[3], the IKEA Effect states that people attribute more value to products they've helped create. In an excerpt from their research, the team describes the results of the experiment:

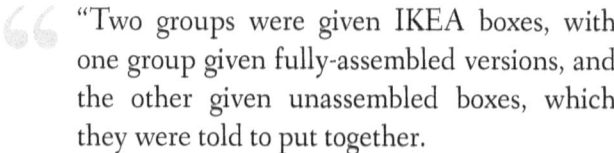 "Two groups were given IKEA boxes, with one group given fully-assembled versions, and the other given unassembled boxes, which they were told to put together.

This second group were willing to pay much more for their box during the subsequent bidding process than those with pre-assembled boxes."

To understand how co-creation impacts business performance, consulting firm Iris created a Participation Brand Index[4]. According to Iris, brands that use co-creation methods "are outperforming the competition without outspending them." The financial return of these companies is strong. For example:

- Investing in the top 20 brands in the Participation Brand Index over three years would have seen 400% higher return on investment than investing in the brands at the bottom of the list.
- Investing in the top 10 brands in the Participation Brand Index over three years would yield a return 200% higher than the S&P 500.

Applying the IKEA effect clearly has financial benefits. Here's how brands are using it in their experiences:

1. Hello Fresh

The most popular meal kit delivery service in the U.S., Hello Fresh sends customers a recipe and ingredients for a delicious meal. Then customers use the kit to cook their dinner. With 2.4 million international subscribers, Hello Fresh has turned meal co-creation into big business[5].

2. LEGO

On their open innovation platform, LEGO IDEAS, the brand gives customers a chance to submit product ideas. The community then votes for their favorites, and LEGO produces the kits. The IDEAS platform is credited with helping turn LEGO into a more culturally relevant and profitable business[6].

3. Build-a-Bear Workshop

Build-a-Bear, a customizable stuffed animal shop, allows children to co-create plush toys. Build-A-Bear has an eight-step personalization process: "Choose Me, Hear Me, Stuff Me, Stitch Me, Fluff Me, Dress Me, Name Me, and Take Me Home."

Harvard researchers Michael I. Norton, Daniel Mochon, and Dan Ariely describe the process this way[7]:

 "Build-a-Bear offers people the 'opportunity' to construct their own teddy bears, charging customers a premium even as they foist assembly costs onto them."

The strategy is clearly working. Build-a-Bear has sold more than 160 million plush animals since the company was founded in 1997[8].

The bottom line

Customer co-creation is proven to make customers value your product, pay more for it, and become more attached to your experience[9]. You don't have to bet the farm on co-creation to see its impact. Instead, run a small experiment using co-creation elements and learn from it. If applied correctly, the IKEA effect can unlock untold value for your brand.

TO APPLY THE IKEA EFFECT, ask yourself:

- If there's a problem area in your product or retail experience, ask yourself if customers can be more involved in the process. Do they feel left out, like there's no transparency, control or participation?
- Are we clearly framing the co-creation as a way for people to add value, and not as a way for the brand to save time or money?
- Can we provide personalization options early in the experience to give customers a sense of ownership?

━━

EIGHTEEN

EMOTIONAL: THE PEAK-END RULE

PEOPLE ONLY REMEMBER YOUR EXPERIENCE BASED ON THE MOST INTENSE POINT, AND THE END

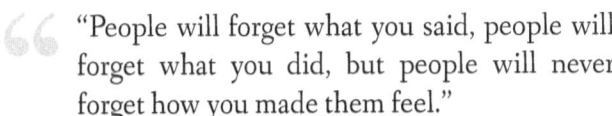 "People will forget what you said, people will forget what you did, but people will never forget how you made them feel."

— Maya Angelou, author and activist

According to Accenture[1], 87% of organizations say traditional experiences no longer satisfy customers. A "good" experience is ok, but for your brand to succeed it needs to stand out. An unforgettable experience means customers talk about it. They recommend it, and they prefer it.

So how do we create an experience that stands out? First, it helps to understand how our brains create memories. Nobel Prize-winning economist Daniel Kahneman explored this subject in a study about how people remember pain[2]. He asked people to rate their discomfort of colonoscopy procedure. Kahneman's team then compared the patients' "remembered" pain experiences with data recorded during the procedure. To their surprise, the team found people rated the pain of the entire experience based on only two points: the intensity of pain at its worst point, and the pain at the end of the procedure.

Kahneman discovered that our brains can't remember everything, so it uses mental shortcuts, called heuristics, to pick out what's important. One of the most important heuristics is emotion. The more intense and more recent the feelings, the more memorable the experience. These principles are the foundation of the so-called peak-end rule[3].

This principle states that people judge an experience based on how they felt at its peak and its end, not the average of every moment of the experience. And that's true whether the experience was good or bad.

This means customers will remember their whole experience based on only two moments — the best (or worst) part of their experience, and the end. That's great news because according to science, there's room for error in your experience. To transform people's memories of your brand, you only have to perfect two moments — the peak and the end.

The peak-end rule is like the 80/20 principle[4] of customer experience. 20% of your experience drives 80% of what people remember. And the more unforgettable the experience, the better the customer. For example:

- **They're loyal.** Customers who had a "very good" experience are 3.5x more likely to repurchase. According to Temkin Group's 2018 research, CX has three components — success, effort, and emotion[5]. They state, "while all three elements impact customer loyalty, an improvement in emotion drives the most significant increase in loyalty."
- **They're advocates.** Customers who had a good experience are 5x more likely to

recommend the company. In fact, there's a 21-point difference in Net Promoter Score[6] between consumers who've had a very good experience with a company and those who've had a very poor experience.

- **They drive revenue.** Temkin also built a model to estimate how "a modest improvement in CX would impact the revenue of a typical $1 billion company across in 20 industries." On average, these companies stand to gain $775 million in value over only three years[7].

Clearly there is financial value to managing customer emotions during the customer experience. But how do the leading brands apply peak-end? Let's take a look at some examples:

1. Chick-fil-A

The drive-thru can be a stressful place. You're not quite sure what you want, there's pressure from the cars behind you, and you're afraid your order will be wrong when you finally get your food. Chick-fil-A has eliminated the most stressful points of the drive-thru by introducing humans. The crew members do this in several ways:

1. They walk over to your car with a tablet when there's a line, therefore reducing the psychological pressure you might feel from other cars.
2. You can ask the crew questions to their face, instead of through a crackling speaker. No more worries about the accuracy of your order.

3. Instead of saying "thank you" the crew ends every customer interaction with the delightful Chick-fil-A trademark phrase, "it's my pleasure."

2. Aldi

At discount grocery chain Aldi, you won't find fancy displays or ornate decorations. The shelves are ugly metal racks stacked with mostly store-brand products. But the most memorable part of Aldi's customer experience? Its lightning-fast checkout process.

Aldi has long been home to the world's fastest checkouts — a huge pain point (and emotional low) in most grocery stores. But because Aldi sells their own products, they can create packaging with multiple barcodes on different panels. Cashiers never have to search for where to scan and rarely look up an item code. They're even scored based on their average checkout time. Aldi has turned an industry pain point into an opportunity to create an unforgettable customer experience.

3. Zappos

The secret to Zappos' success lies in how they handle the number one challenge of buying shoes online — what to do do if they don't fit? Zappos allows customers to return anything they've ordered for free, up to 365 days after the item was ordered. That includes shoes that have been worn, broken, or that customers wore for 364 days and decided they didn't like anymore. Because of their liberal return policy, Zappos quickly built a thriving business.

In this case, the peak and end of an experience are tied

to the same moment — returning an item. Knowing that Zappos happily takes returns created brand advocates, drove trial, and increased repeat customers.

The bottom line

Experience design projects take a lot of time, money, and effort to complete. They're rarely small and always cross departments. That means lots of stakeholders, which translates to lots of resistance. But the great thing about peak-end is that you can start applying it to your strategy now. Find the biggest pain point in your customer journey. Transform it, and you won't just improve that moment, you'll enhance your entire experience.

TO APPLY THE PEAK-END RULE, ask yourself:

- Where do our customers feel the best, and the worst, in our experience? What touchpoints are they interacting with at this point? Are they waiting on something, like a food order?
- Where does our experience actually end? If you're an e-commerce brand, that might be different places for different customers. For example, if someone returns a product their experience ends in a different place from someone who didn't need to mail back any returns.
- Do we have a clear customer or user journey map that measures our customers' emotional journey? If not, now would be a great time to create one.

PART SEVEN
THE C.H.O.I.C.E. MODEL IN ACTION

EXAMPLES AND USE CASES

In this section, we'll walk through four examples that illustrate how major brands apply all six principles of the C.H.O.I.C.E. model. I'll demonstrate how these principles help each company create outstanding customer experiences, and when applicable show the associated return on investment.

The purpose of this section is not only to demonstrate C.H.O.I.C.E. in action, but to give you tangible examples that can help spur thoughts about improving and optimizing your own experience. My hope is by seeing specific examples, you'll be inspired to apply these principles yourself. As Dale Carnegie said:

"Learning is an active process. We learn by doing. Only knowledge that is used sticks in your mind."

NINETEEN

HOW NETFLIX APPLIES C.H.O.I.C.E.

> "If the Starbucks secret is a smile when you get your latte, [Netflix's secret] is that the Website adapts to the individual's taste."
>
> - Reed Hastings, co-founder and CEO of Netflix

Founded in 1997 by Reed Hastings and Marc Randolph, Netflix began as a service that allowed people to rent DVDs online. Many of us remember getting Netflix's distinctive red envelopes in the mail. After we finished watching our DVDs, we dropped them into a return envelope and mailed them back. This simple experience and the "no late fees guarantee" quickly destroyed Blockbuster's dominance of the rental market.

But as their customer base grew, Netflix knew it couldn't rest on its laurels. In the year 2000, they introduced a personalized recommendation algorithm to suggest new DVDs based on a customer's previous rentals. In 2007, Netflix began their transition from DVD-only to a video streaming service. Now, Netflix is synonymous with excellent customer experience. It's become the defacto entertainment source for many. So much so that 15% of the world's total web traffic[1] goes to Netflix, and the company has 167 million customers across the globe.[2]

The most significant customer pain point, and the challenge that Netflix's experience aims to solve, is choice overload. We've all found ourselves trapped in the "eternal scroll," searching through Netflix and unable to find something to watch. In an experience like this, matching the right content to the right customer is critical. As Netflix researchers Chris Alvino and Justin Basilico put it[3]:

> "A problem we face is that our catalog contains many more videos than can be displayed on a single page, and each member comes with their own unique set of interests."

So how does Netflix rise to this challenge? They discover what works through real-world field experimentation, built on proven psychological and behavioral science principles - conscious or not. At any given time, Netflix is testing dozens of hypotheses in front of live customers. As the Netflix Tech Blog put it[4]:

> "Every product change Netflix considers goes through a rigorous A/B testing process before becoming the default user experience."

Because Netflix is a digital subscription service, its design teams can quickly discover which tests are working and which ones aren't. In this chapter, we'll unlock the scientific principle underlying the Netflix customer experience, through the lens of the C.H.O.I.C.E. model.

━━━

Clear: Is the Netflix experience salient and simple for customers to understand?

The biggest challenge for Netflix is getting the right information to customers fast and making that information easy to understand and engaging. The Netflix Technology Blog puts it this way:

> "Broadly, we know that if you don't capture a member's attention within **90 seconds**, that member will likely lose interest and move onto another activity."[5]

Netflix uses several psychological principles to create a simple, salient experience that hooks customers right away - the top-10 effect, and the picture superiority effect.

As discussed in our chapter on salience bias, the top-10 effect states that people prefer to group information into round-numbers, and then classify everything outside of that group as inferior. Netflix's "Top 10" feature takes advantage of this bias, and customers' eyes are immediately drawn to it.

The picture superiority effect states that images are more salient than words. Although we briefly covered Netflix's use of this effect earlier in the book, we will explore this in more depth here.

As we know, the Netflix experience is image-driven. Thumbnail images are one of the main variables tested on the platform. The images have to get people to select a title but without misrepresenting the story. Netflix's tech team described it this way[6]:

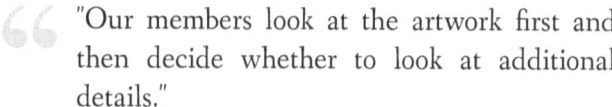 "Our members look at the artwork first and then decide whether to look at additional details."

Netflix was an early pioneer of thumbnail optimization for digital environments. Originally, Netflix would just use the general-purpose images provided by the studios. Many of these images were resized billboards or print ads, not suitable for a digital experience[7]. So Netflix began creating and testing different thumbnails to see if they could match the right audience to the right content. Eventually, not only did Netflix learn what images performed best, they created a requirements list for a compelling thumbnail: a background image, a title treatment, a "new episode" badge, and a Netflix logo for original content. The tech team discovered three insights about well-performing thumbnail images:

1. Faces conveying emotion that align with the title's genre perform strongly. For example, showing a close-up of a screaming woman's face for a horror film, or a laughing woman for a comedy.
2. When a thumbnail features a famous or "polarizing" character, it performs better. For example, showing the villain Voldemort's face would likely work as well as showing Harry Potter's on a thumbnail.
3. Different images do better in different parts of the world. Therefore artwork testing and image delivery need to be localized.

Netflix's ability to serve relevant, adaptable and image-driven content means its experience is second-to-none when it comes to salience and simplicity for customers.

———

Holistic: Does Netflix's "big picture" experience set up individual interactions to succeed?

The first element of a holistic experience, the mere exposure effect, is about getting the brand's codes - images, words, sounds, and logos - firmly embedded in customer's minds. That way, when people interact with the experience it's set-up for success. Netflix, being a first-mover in streaming, has taken this early advantage and run with it. For example, most people can recognize the Netflix "N" logo, their distinctive red and black brand colors, and the "badum" sound that indicates the app has launched. The brand plays with its codes by launching advertising campaigns like "Netflix is a joke". Even cultural concepts like "Netflix and chill", or changing your streaming password as the ultimate act of revenge on an ex, show that the brand is firmly embedded in this generation's subconscious. All of these visual, sonic, and cultural elements work to prime customers as well. By setting the stage with sensory cues, Netflix gets you ready to binge.

After customers stream a title, confirmation bias comes in the way of industry accolades. Their awards season strategy is taken straight from HBO's playbook. Just as HBO found that dominating television award season made their channel seem more prestigious and therefore more desired by customers, Netflix knows that Oscar, BAFTA, and Emmy wins translate to subscribers. If Netflix recommends a movie that a customer watches and enjoys, then that movie goes on to win the Best Picture Oscar, they feel vindicated. The customer's ego is comforted, knowing that they took a risk, enjoyed a movie, told their friends, and the Oscars confirmed they made the "right choice" by choosing Netflix.

———

Open: Does the Netflix experience make it clear what's happening now, why, and what's to come?

Because Netflix is a digital experience, it can be difficult to show customers what's happening behind the scenes. However, Netflix considers transparency around personalization an essential part of its experience. Their technology research team put it this way[8]:

> "[Awareness of how the platform is using customer data] not only promotes trust in the system but encourages members to give feedback that will result in better recommendations."

So how does Netflix promote that awareness? By providing explanations as to why they've recommended a specific title to a customer. Netflix states[9]:

> "We are not recommending [the title] because it suits our business needs, but because it matches the information we have from you: your explicit taste preferences and ratings,

your viewing history, or even your friends'
recommendations."

Clearly, providing an open experience are important to
Netflix.

———

Individual: Does the Netflix experience use relevant data
to personalize?

Netflix describes itself as "customer-obsessed" and strives to
deliver a one-to-one experience. It's no secret that much of
its competitive advantage comes from its ability to personalize content. Netflix's "Top Picks" category is a prime
example of this philosophy in action. More than 80% of
Netflix titles customers watched in the last two years have
been as a direct result of its recommendation engine - not
someone searching for a specific piece of content[10].

One of Netflix's most significant assets is its data.
Knowing who watches what content has given the company
incredible insight into their customers' minds. We just
discussed how Netflix began personalizing their thumbnail
images for large groups of its customers. However, growth in
its customer base and increased personalization ability gave
Netflix the ability to create "100 million different products,
with one for each of [their] members."[11] They began
designing personalized thumbnails for new content based
on insights from individual customer data. For example, if a
customer watched a few movies that feature actor Paul
Bettany, and *Avengers Endgame* was newly released to
Netflix (in which Bettany plays the character Vision), the

system could show a thumbnail for *Avengers Endgame* that prominently featured Vision's face.

Another way Netflix creates an individual experience is by ranking their content. The ranking system decides in what order titles will be shown. Netflix states that its goal is to "find the best possible ordering of a set of items for a member, within a specific context, in real-time.[12]" Combined with unique thumbnails for each individual these rankings help create an experience that's truly "individual".

Contextual: Does the context of Netflix's experience subtly guide customer choice?

To encourage users to pick a title, Netflix employs a combination of defaults and a principle called idleness aversion. It states that people are happier when they are busier, even if forced to be busy. To accomplish this, Netflix gives people visual information with which to engage. For example, their home page experience forces users to watch trailers that auto-play by default when they dwell on the title. This feature is a source of frustration for many people, but the benefits of Idleness Aversion have clearly outweighed the costs for Netflix.

To create a contextual experience that persuades people to subscribe, Netflix applies a principle known as reciprocity. Reciprocity is a social norm of responding to a positive action with another positive action. It's why you feel indebted when someone does you a favor. Made famous by Robert Cialdini in his book *Influence*, reciprocity can be summed by the saying, "You've got to give to get."

To understand how best to apply the reciprocity principle, Netflix asked their customer base, " What one thing would you like to know more about before signing up for Netflix"? The most popular answer was "knowing all of the movies and TV shows available.[13]" In response, Netflix experimented with showing customers available content on the home page. But their experiment revealed something interesting. Showing customers too much of the content was distracting. Many of them browsed but never signed up. So Netflix redesigned their experiment. Designers still used the Reciprocity Principle, but this time they used an image that hinted at an extensive catalog. But they didn't let customers browse the whole thing. Giving people a sneak peek — but not the total view — made customers more likely to sign up for a free streaming trial.

Emotional: Do customers have positive emotions and memories associated with the Netflix experience?

The emotional power of Netflix's experience comes mainly from its content. The peak-end rule applies to any good story. The emotional ups and downs of a movie and a satisfying ending are out of Netflix's control, but it does incentivize them to suggest and create strong content. Netflix knows if its algorithm can match you with the right title, the emotional bond with Netflix will grow from there. It's a type of IKEA effect. By deciding on something to watch, the user and Netflix co-create an emotional experience.

The bottom line

In the past decade, the Netflix site has undergone an incredible transformation. These changes and optimizations were made possible because of a design culture built on the principles of "test and learn." Navin Iyengar, Lead Product Designer, described the Netflix testing philosophy[14] this way:

 "A lot of the UX ideas we have are A/B tested, so we can understand what effect they have on member acquisition or satisfaction around the world.

The results of those experiments help keep us focused on the most important things to work on."

At the end of the day, we believe A/B testing yields the most reliable information for us to understand what people want out of our service."

A culture of experimentation is critical for psychological principles to be implemented in any organization. There's no magic button you can press to make your culture data and experiment-driven. It's a tough process that requires designers to work closely with marketing, product, IT, operations, and digital teams. But, if implemented correctly, the potential upside is huge.

TWENTY

HOW UBER APPLIES C.H.O.I.C.E.

 "I think Uber is just very different; there's no model to copy."

- Travis Kalanick, founder of Uber

Founded in 2009 by Garrett Camp and Travis Kalanick, Uber started as the answer to a simple question, "what if you could request a trip from your phone?"[1] Now available in 600 cities spread across 65 countries with more than 75 million users, for many people Uber has become the default choice for travel. The company quickly expanded beyond Uber, adding UberX, UberBLACK, UberPool, and Uber Eats within a few years. The scale and speed of adoption have been incredible, and Uber cites its unique business model and user experience as the reason for this rapid growth.

To keep its business model humming, Uber must manage a delicate balance between two parties: drivers (also called couriers by the Uber Eats business) and riders. The secret to Uber's seamless experience hinges on balancing driver supply and rider demand. To keep both sides of their equation in harmony, Uber runs experiments that utilize psychology and behavior science principles.

The biggest customer pain point — waiting for a ride

Imagine you're outside at 2 am on a winter night, waiting for your Uber while shivering on a dark street in a strange town. Or you're late for an important meeting that you *just might make* if your Uber is on time. In these high-pressure situations, your perception of time is warped. Every second takes a minute. Every minute takes an hour. Your emotions are running high, so an experience where you wait too long for a ride is disproportionately disappointing.

The biggest driver pain point — spending too much time driving while not making enough money

Uber drivers are independent contractors. That means they can set their own hours and availability, and Uber gets to lower their labor costs because they have fewer "employees" on the books. But the benefits of an independent workforce comes at a price. Because Uber can't require drivers to work at a particular time or place, the company is at constant risk of not being able to meet rider demand. Drivers work for Uber for many reasons - flexibility, freedom, or maybe they just like to meet new people. But most drivers share a goal to make as much money in as little time as possible. The company balances their need for drivers to work longer with the driver's motivation to make more money by using psychology to educate, incentivize, and encourage workers to stay on the clock for longer.

In this case study, we'll mainly focus on the rider's experience as this is the one most people are familiar with. We'll use the C.H.O.I.C.E. model to examine how the company uses psychology and behavioral science to create an industry-defining experience.

Clear: Is the Uber experience salient and simple for both riders and drivers to understand?

Behind the scenes, the Uber business is incredibly complicated. The magic of the experience relies on creating an app that's simple to use and salient. Features like automatic location detection ensure that Uber doesn't ask too much of its users. At any given time, customers only see three to four pieces of information on the screen, with salient action elements such as "submit" and "cancel" buttons. The overall feel of the Uber app is one of lightness and speed - it loads quickly and an Uber can be hailed with very little effort.

When customer pain points are found, Uber is quick to address them. For instance, in 2016, the brand's user research group found that riders were irritated because they expected drivers to know where they were without dropping a pin. This resulted in frustration until Uber developed "Rendevous", a redesign of their pickup experience. Simon Pan, a designer who worked on the project, described Rendevous this way[2]:

 "Uber finds you the optimal meeting place based on who you are, where you are, and where you're going. Uber saves you time without you needing to select a pickup.

People-friendly walking instructions help

you better understand and identify your meeting spot. No more nonsensical addresses."

Uber's fundamental design principles of simplicity, salience, and focus come through in every part of their app experience.

━━━

Holistic: Does Uber's "big picture" experience set up individual interactions to succeed?

The holistic experience of Uber is one of speed and convenience. Everything about the brand, including its service extensions like Uber Eats, is synonymous with ease of use. Even its name has become embedded in the culture as a way to describe a disrupted industry. The so-called "uberfi-cation" of a market is another way of saying its been transformed by a crowdsourced, flexible workforce. As psychologist and consumer behavior specialist Dr. Paul Marsden described it[3]:

> "Uber, the on-demand 'driver for hire' mobile service has become the poster-child for digital disruption, delivering... better value to consumers than legacy taxis. And so digital innovators are seeking to 'uberfy' the world with convenient on-demand mobile services... that digitally match demand with supply.
>
> Tap your phone, get service."

By attaching its name to a variety of new businesses,

Uber has created a reputation that primes customers to expect a seamless service that is then confirmed by their experience.

———

Open: Does Uber's experience make it clear what's happening now, why, and what's to come?

In order to create an open experience, Uber keeps users informed. They provide key information to make it clear where the customer is headed, and when they will arrive at their destination. The Uber app also provides information on how arrival times are calculated. This provides customers transparency but doesn't overwhelm a non-technical audience with too many details. They state:

- "Before a trip starts, your app provides an ETA for when your driver should arrive at your pickup location.
- After your trip starts, your app provides an ETA for when you should arrive at your destination.
- Please note that ETA times are estimates and not guaranteed. A variety of external factors like heavy traffic or road construction can impact travel time.
- Before you request a ride, your app displays a time in the black SET PICKUP LOCATION bar. This time estimates how long nearby drivers should take to arrive at your pickup location.
- Using the slider at the bottom of your screen,

you can view the ETA for each vehicle option available in your city.

- After a trip starts, your app will continually update the ETA for your destination."

Since the biggest pain point for riders is waiting for their Uber, the company needs to make time pass more quickly. To do this, Uber uses a car animation on a map to indicate progress. This application of the goal gradient effect is interesting because it isn't driving customers to complete a checkout process or finish filling out their dating profile. Instead, this use of the goal gradient can change customer perceptions of time by providing transparency. The closer your Uber gets to you, the faster the time seems to pass.

To keep cars on the road, and the Uber ecosystem balanced, the driver app also applies the goal gradient effect. When drivers are ready to log-off for the day, they get a message that they're close to hitting their target income. But the company is careful to balance this psychological trigger with making obvious how to quit driving for the day. As Michael Amodeo, an Uber spokesman, told the New York Times in 2017[4],

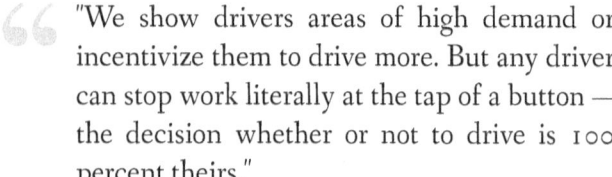

"We show drivers areas of high demand or incentivize them to drive more. But any driver can stop work literally at the tap of a button — the decision whether or not to drive is 100 percent theirs."

Uber is also open about another piece of critical user data - riders' star rating. Mysterious but powerful, the rating system dictates how quickly users can get an Uber, how many drivers will be willing to pick them up, and if they're allowed to keep using the app[5]. The Uber website is clear about what riders need to do to maintain five-star status[6]:

1. "Short wait times - Be ready to go when [drivers] arrive at the pickup location. Be sure the location you entered is actually where you'll be.
2. Courtesy - Treat drivers and their cars the way they'd expect to be treated themselves.
3. Safety - Drivers want to make sure everyone in their car is safe, and shouldn't feel pressured to break any laws."

By maintaining an open experience, Uber keeps both riders and drivers happy, safe, and satisfied.

Individual: Does the Uber experience use relevant data to personalize?

Uber uses multiple data sources to create an "individual" experience. For example, its dynamic pricing algorithm changes the cost of a ride based on a variety of factors. The algorithm uses environmental and historical customer data to determine how much to charge for a ride. For example, the price will change depending on the time of day, how many other people are requesting rides, the weather, and local events near you. Uber can also pull behavioral data for individual users. This could include patterns of traveling to certain places at certain times and how much you were willing to pay for your last trip. In fact, Uber will charge you more if their algorithm thinks you're willing to pay more.[7]

Although Uber's "individual experience" can sometimes result in high prices, it also creates maximum value for drivers. If rides are in high demand, it makes sense that higher prices would incentivize more drivers to work during those times. That way, there are more available Ubers for willing riders. Ideally, Uber's individual experience works in both the rider and the driver's favor, while maintaining the critical balance between supply and demand.

———

Contextual: Does the context of Uber's experience subtly guide rider and driver choices?

To create a contextual experience, Uber employs a variety of psychological and behavioral science principles. For example, loss aversion helps keep drivers on the road and supply high. When drivers are about to log-off for the day, they get a message that employs loss aversion tactics. The app states, "You're $10 away from making $330 in net earnings. Are you sure you want to go offline?" The driver app then uses the power of defaults to keep drivers on the road. Below the loss aversion message, there are two prompts: "Go offline" and "Keep driving." The text "keep driving" is already highlighted[8]. It's not clear how long this feature keeps drivers on the road, but even if it's only for a few rides during peak hours, the financial power of this default has paid off.

The cashless effect is another contextual experience principle that's proven valuable for Uber. The app removes the pain of payment completely, creating a system that makes customers willing to pay more for their ride because they don't have to have the cash on hand to pay for it.

On the rider side, the app uses social proof as a way to incentivize good behavior. The infamous Uber rating is a way for drivers to provide fellow workers guidance on what kind of behavior they can expect from this user. The higher the rating, the stronger the social proof.

Emotional: Do customers have positive emotions and memories associated with the Uber experience?

Waiting for an Uber can be an emotional experience in itself. Being late for a critical business meeting or not making an international flight can be life-altering. In these high-pressure situations, people's perception of time is warped. Every second takes a minute, every minute takes an hour. Not only that, but people will use this warped wait-time to judge their entire customer experience. Why? It's all down to the peak-end rule.

As you'll recall, customers remember their whole experience based on only two moments—the best (or worst) part of their experience and the end. Because wait times are the key to a great customer experience, Uber's behavioral science team has spent countless hours[9] addressing this pain point. In their research, the group discovered three key principles dealing with how people perceive wait times: idleness aversion, operational transparency, and the goal gradient effect. Earlier in this case study, we addressed how Uber uses these effects to manage both the peak and the end of their experience.

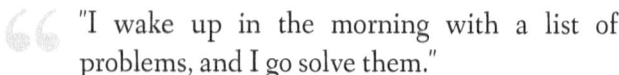

The bottom line

There's no doubt that a large part of Uber's revenue comes from optimizing their experience using science. For instance, when an experiment was run with Uber Pool that applied operational transparency and the goal gradient effect, the results were impressive[10]:

> "The Express POOL team tested these ideas in an A/B experiment and observed an 11 percent reduction in the post-request cancellation rate."

If you want to apply psychological and behavioral science principles to your brand, a testing mentality is critical. You have to be willing to test the application of the same principle in hundreds of different ways before discovering the best solution.

This experimentation mentality comes from the top down at Uber. As co-founder Travis Kalanick said:

> "I wake up in the morning with a list of problems, and I go solve them."

TWENTY-ONE

HOW DISNEY APPLIES C.H.O.I.C.E.

 It's in our best interest to put some of the old rules aside and create new ones and follow the consumer - what the consumer wants and where the consumer wants to go."

- Bob Iger, Executive Chairman of The Walt Disney Company

Started in 1923, the Walt Disney Company began life as the Disney Brothers Cartoon Studio. Founded by brothers Walt and Roy, Disney was an early leader in the animation industry but quickly diversified into film production, television, merchandising, and theme parks. In this case study, we will focus on the Walt Disney World Resort customer experience.

The biggest customer pain point - overwhelming choice

Although Disney World is known as "The Most Magical Place on Earth," there are still pain points to fix. Primarily, choice overload. As Thomas Staggs, former Chief Operating Officer of the company put it[1]:

"Walt Disney World is vast. There's more to do than you could do in a month. That choice is overwhelming."

It's a customer experience paradox - Disney's guests visit the park because there's so much to do. But they can leave the park disappointed because there's *too much* to do. When you reduce most customer issues at Disney World down to basics, they're about managing choice.

From a business perspective, Disney World has a mix of aspirations. Like Starbucks, they want to create an enchanting experience. Like Uber, Disney wants to be transparent, but must be careful about which parts of the experience they show (after all, the surest way to kill a magic trick is to see how it was done). And like Netflix, Disney leverages personalization to help customers navigate choice. As Staggs put it,

"I can't think of a business that isn't affected by more choice and more access to information and an increasing desire for personalization [than Disney World]."

In this case study, we'll use the C.H.O.I.C.E. model to breakdown the psychology and behavioral science behind Disney World's industry-leading experience. We'll examine how Disney uses these science-based approaches (consciously or not) to turn overwhelming choice into a magical experience.

Clear: Is the Disney World experience salient and simple for people to understand?

Salient and simple experiences are created through a state of "cognitive ease." That means Disney has to take a complex vacation planning process and make it so simple that it's fun. Their "overwhelming choice" pain point means Disney has to make sure the right information is salient and easy to understand for guests. Disney accomplishes this by talking to users in plain language, distilling a complex process into simple steps, and personalizing the experience as much as possible.

For example, when customers register for "My Disney Experience," the brand's online booking portal, there's a single sign-on that works across all Disney companies. Customers who already have a Disney+ streaming service, or have booked a Disney cruise in the past don't have to create a new profile to book a trip to Disney World. Instead, they can log-in with their existing username and password. For customers, it's easier not to remember one more password. And from a business perspective, single sign-on provides amazing data-mining and personalization potential. For instance, Disney could identify customers who watch Star Wars content on Disney+, then suggest Star Wars rides and areas of the park when these customers book their Disney World vacation.

"My Disney Experience" also eliminates all corporate speak in favor of plain language. For example, the entire vacation booking process is distilled to five easy steps, and each one is translated for customers. These steps and their meanings are:

1. Family and Friends = "Who's going?"

2. Resort Hotel = "Are you staying with us?"
3. Park Tickets = "Have tickets?"
4. Dining = "We accept reservations through the following date."
5. FastPass+ = "Get a ticket"

This language makes it easy for customers to understand exactly what's required of them.

———

Holistic: Does Disney's "big picture" experience set up individual interactions to succeed?

The Walt Disney Company has spent nearly 100 years building and solidifying brand codes, images, sounds, jingles, colors, and content. Disney has created a universe of entertainment synonymous with American culture. The mere exposure effect certainly comes into play for kids and parents before they decide to visit the park. Priming is also used heavily by Disney in millions of movie theaters, tablets and television sets. By the time guests get to the park, they're ready to be swept off their feet by the magic of Disney World. And once guests have left, the company subtly pushes them to check out ShopDisney, the brand's online store. There's a whole world of Disney branded content in which kids and parents can immerse themselves post-visit, including toys, outfits, games, apps, lunchboxes, movies, and shows. Disney are the kings of corporate synergy.

———

Open: Does the Disney World experience make it clear what's happening now, why, and what's to come?

How does Disney World balance transparency and magic? The Imagineers at Disney are experts in knowing what elements to show and what parts to hide. For instance, Disney World's online booking system is simple to use. Customers can see exactly where they are in the booking process, what's left to do, and how much everything will cost. Once they're in the park, the "My Disney Experience" app is like a personal tour guide. You can order food, find wait times for specific rides, buy FastPass+, and see exactly where you are in the park.

But as you walk down the street at Disney, you'd never guess that there's a whole world of underground tunnels called utilidors beneath you[2]. These tunnels connect all the areas of the park and help maintenance staff and cast members - the folks dressed up like Mickey Mouse and Donald Duck - to get around without being seen. Even garbage cans use a system of pressurized tubes connected to the bottom of each bin[3]. This way, guests only see the most "magical" parts of the experience - never a cast member smoking a cigarette on their break, or an overflowing trash bin. This balance of openness and mystery helps make Disney World a truly magical experience.

Individual: Does the Disney World experience use relevant data to personalize?

 "Technology is lifting the limits of creativity and transforming the possibilities for entertainment and leisure."

- Bob Iger, Chairman & CEO, Disney

DISNEY HAS TAKEN the promise of data and technology to heart. The MagicBand, combined with the "My Disney Experience" app, and the FastPass+ system that allows customers to skip park lines, is a prime example of using data to create an individual experience.

As discussed in our chapter on the cashless effect, Disney's MagicBand is an "all-in-one device that effortlessly connects you to all [your] vacation choices." An internet-of-things connected bracelet, the device removes friction all over the park. Guests can pay for items without cash, get into their hotel room, even be recognized by Disney characters and greeted by name. MagicBands also give the company insight into where guests are spending money, what they're buying, what they're riding, and where they're spending time in the park.

Disney uses MagicBand data to create an individual experience in many ways. For instance, seeing where customers shop and what they buy means Disney can deliver offers, gifts, and experiences that match guest preferences. Disney World staff can use live data to see where guests are congregating in the park, or spending too long waiting for a ride[4]. The park operations team can then deploy distractions, in the form of parades or real-time incentives, to change locations. When guests use FastPass+ in combination with MagicBands, they get individual itineraries, optimized by machine learning so that they can visit the maximum number of attractions.

The MagicBand is only one part of Disney's holistic strategy to transform their company through customer data. Their four stated aims are[5]:

1. Drive operational efficiency with a data-driven approach
2. Enhance interactions across channels with a range of digital tools
3. Transform the customer experience with analytics and wearable tech
4. Increase personalization with connected products

Their large investment in MagicBand and its associated personalization projects have begun to bear fruit. Disney World can now accommodate 3,000 more daily visits, a million more guests a year, billions in profit, and a personalized customer experience[6].

Contextual: Does the context of Disney's experience subtly guide customer choice?

It's clear that Disney methodically considers the psychological environment and mechanics of a contextual experience. For example, the MagicBand is one the best examples of the cashless effect in action. Meg Crofton, president of the Walt Disney World Resort at the time of its development, started the project with the aim of eliminating all the friction for guests. As Crofton told Wired magazine[7]:

> "We were looking for pain points. What are the barriers to getting into the experience faster?"

Not only do MagicBands reduce the pain of payment for customers, but they also reduce all friction points in the park. This makes room for a better overall customer experience. MagicBands allow employees to "move past transactions into an interactive space, where they can personalize the experience" as Crofton put it.

Another example of Disney World creating a contextual experience is by applying defaults. For instance, Disney worked with researchers to test whether healthy default options would make a difference in getting children to eat better in the park. They found that 47.9% of visitors stuck with the default healthy side, and 66.3% kept the lighter beverage selection. This approach went live in fast food and sit-down restaurants across the park.[8]

Emotional: Do customers have positive emotions and memories associated with the Disney World experience?

Creating happy memories at Disney World shouldn't be hard. But not even the happiest place on earth is without its challenges. By the end of a one-week vacation spent in the Florida sun, guests can feel exhausted and stressed out. So why is Disney World able to conjure good memories for guests? As we learned by studying the peak-end rule, the end of an experience is disproportionately important to creating good memories. So how is that possible if the end of a vacation is usually such a downer?

Because Disney knows that leaving the park isn't the end of the guest experience. The pictures taken in the park and shared on social media are the actual "end" of the peak-end. It's the memories themselves that Disney has to shape.

So how do they do this? One way is through the design of the park itself, so that it looks better in photos. In fact, Kodak and Disney conducted an intense study to understand what colors would make better backgrounds in photographs[9]. The study revealed how to strategically apply colors to the paths and surroundings to enhance guest photos, thereby making their memories seem happier and more vivid.

Disney World not only manages the ends of their experience to perfection, they manage the customer conversations around them as well. The brand is the second most popular on social media[10], and is well-known for re-sharing customer posts about their favorite moments in the park. By lending some of its social media shine to park visitors, Disney makes the magic last even longer.

The bottom line

Walt Disney World is a proven leader in creating experiences visitors love. It didn't happen by chance - Disney's culture and processes have made them undisputed masters of experience design. In fact, in 1987, former President of Imagineering Marty Sklar formalized Walt Disney's original guiding principles. Sklar called them "Mickey's 10

Commandments", and they serve as timeless guidance for anyone aiming to create a stellar customer experience[11].

Mickey's 10 Commandments

1. "Know your audience - Don't bore people, talk down to them, or lose them by assuming that they know what you know.
2. Wear your guest's shoes - Insist that designers, staff, and your board members experience your facility as visitors as often as possible.
3. Organize the flow of people and ideas: Use good storytelling techniques, tell good stories, not lectures. Layout your exhibit with clear logic.
4. Create a weenie: Lead visitors from one area to another by creating visual magnets and giving visitors rewards for making the journey
5. Communicate with visual literacy: Make good use of all the non-verbal ways of communication - color, shape, form, texture.
6. Avoid overload: Resist the temptation to tell too much, to have too many objects, don't force people to swallow more than they can digest, try to stimulate and provide guidance to those who want more.
7. Tell one story at a time: If you have a lot of information divide it into distinct, logical, organized stories, people can absorb and retain information more clearly if the path to the next concept is clear and logical.
8. Avoid contradiction: Clear institutional identity helps give you the competitive edge. The public

needs to know who you are and what
differentiates you from other institutions they
may have seen.

9. For every ounce of treatment, provide a ton of
   fun: How do you woo people from all other
   temptations? Give people plenty of opportunity
   to enjoy themselves by emphasizing ways that
   let people participate in the experience and by
   making your environment rich and appealing to
   all senses.

10. Keep it up: Never underestimate the
    importance of cleanliness and routine
    maintenance; people expect to get a good show
    every time, people will comment more on
    broken and dirty stuff."

TWENTY-TWO

HIDDEN DANGERS OF APPLYING
BEHAVIORAL SCIENCE

 "Whenever I'm asked to autograph a copy of
Nudge... I sign it, "Nudge for good."

Unfortunately, that is meant as a plea, not an
expectation."

- Richard H. Thaler

Right now, you're probably saying to yourself, "This sounds
pretty good! I can use behavioral science to get customers to
do whatever I want them to. It's just a matter of applying it
in the right way." But before we get ahead of ourselves, it's
worth flagging some risks to applying behavioral science:

1. Belief in the law of small numbers

Kahneman and Tversky used this term to describe people's
tendency to make generalizations based on small amounts
of data. This is something everyone does, including trained
statisticians.

Be wary of betting the farm on experiments with small sample sizes. When a trial is successful, continue to test it in different environments that mirror your customer base as much as possible. That way, you can make sure your intervention works across a representative sample of people before rolling it out to a large portion of your customers.

2. Behavioral science interventions can backfire

Consider the case of United Airlines, who restructured their yearly bonus scheme as a lottery[1]. Rather than give a smaller cash payment to everyone, United entered all of their employees in a draw for a big prize. For example, instead of a $5,000 annual raise, an employee might have their name entered in a lottery for a chance to win a Mercedes worth $75,000.

United reframed their annual bonus into what they felt would be a more attractive payoff. But they failed to consider the powerful loss aversion principle: People are happier with a small guaranteed payoff than with a chance at a much bigger prize.

To say United's experiment went poorly would be an understatement. Within days of announcing the plan, United was forced to withdraw the lottery and return to their previous financial payout scheme.

3. Ethical concerns

 "There's no such thing as neutral design"

- Richard H. Thaler

When designing experiences, there are moments where you're pressured to produce results. It's what our careers are built on, and how we advance. But at a certain point, you may find your ethical boundaries being tested. You can't produce results at all costs while maintaining moral integrity. It's worthwhile to reflect on a personal code of conduct for combining behavioral science and experience design, before finding yourself in a worrying situation.

Designer Joe Leech outlined his moral compass in his post, "UX ethics and having a code of conduct[2]." Leech abides by the following when designing digital customer experiences:

1. Don't trick
2. Don't cheat
3. Don't lie
4. Provide positive benefit

In response to the many organizations that have started applying behavioral science, Richard Thaler has an ethical code he prescribes[3]. He states:

1. "All nudging should be transparent and never misleading.
2. It should be as easy as possible to opt out of the nudge preferably with as little as one mouse click.
3. There should be good reason to believe that the behavior being encouraged will improve the welfare of those being nudged."

There are behavioral science and psychology principles,

that when rigorously applied, can be perceived as a "psychological trick" you're playing on customers. It's up to every professional to decide where that line is for themselves, and a personal code of conduct is a great place to start.

PART EIGHT
BONUS MATERIALS

TWENTY-THREE

7 BOOKS THAT WILL CHANGE THE WAY YOU THINK ABOUT EXPERIENCE

Those who design experiences must understand how to inspire customers to action. But you can't inspire people if you don't understand how they think. The books below represent a solid foundation of psychology and behavioral science knowledge from which to build better experiences. These are the best behavioral science and psychology books for designers, marketers, and customer experience managers — anyone who manages touchpoints, interaction design, or the customer journey itself.

1. 100 Things Every Designer Needs to Know About People, by Susan Weinschenk

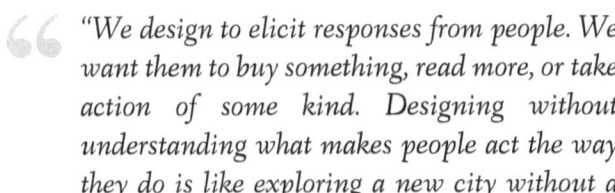

"We design to elicit responses from people. We want them to buy something, read more, or take action of some kind. Designing without understanding what makes people act the way they do is like exploring a new city without a

> *map: results will be haphazard, confusing, and inefficient."*

100 Things Ever Designer Needs to Know About People combines science, research, and practical use cases to create a fantastic guide to designing smarter experiences. A collection of well-researched principles that provides deep insight into customer psychology as it relates to experience design.

2. Thinking, Fast and Slow, by Daniel Kahneman

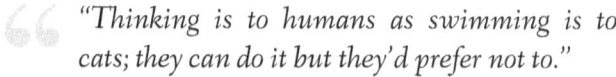 *"Thinking is to humans as swimming is to cats; they can do it but they'd prefer not to."*

Nobel laureate Daniel Kahneman conducts a deep dive into the biases and psychological principles that drive people's behavior. Kahneman introduces the dual process model of System 1 (fast) and System 2 (slow) thinking.

3. The Paradox of Choice, by Barry Schwartz

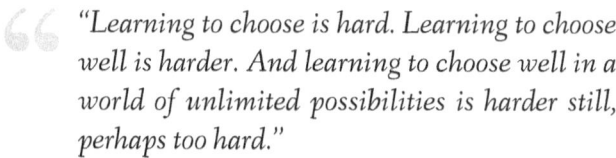 *"Learning to choose is hard. Learning to choose well is harder. And learning to choose well in a world of unlimited possibilities is harder still, perhaps too hard."*

In this book, researcher Barry Schwartz explores how people make decisions in a world overcrowded with options. Schwartz introduces the science-backed idea that less choice can make a big impact on everyone's behavior and happiness.

4. Psychology for Designers, by Joe Leech

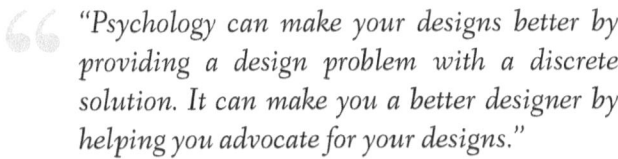

> *"Psychology can make your designs better by providing a design problem with a discrete solution. It can make you a better designer by helping you advocate for your designs."*

In this tactical guide, author Joe Leech walks the reader through the process of researching and applying psychology to design. From the basics of what psychology is, to how to apply specific principles, this is a great end-to-end guide for designers of any level.

5. Nudge: Improving Decisions about Health, Wealth, and Happiness, by Richard H. Thaler and Cass R. Sunstein

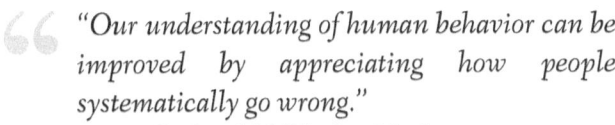

> *"Our understanding of human behavior can be improved by appreciating how people systematically go wrong."*
> *— Richard H. Thaler, Nudge*

The book that launched a thousand ad agency "Nudge Units", this is a well-written and easy read that introduces the concept of "nudging"—using science to arrange the environment so that people are more likely to choose a certain option or behavior.

6. Hooked: How to Build Habit-Forming Products, by Nir Eyal

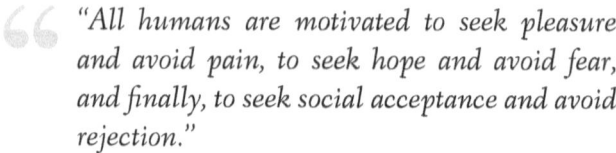 *"All humans are motivated to seek pleasure and avoid pain, to seek hope and avoid fear, and finally, to seek social acceptance and avoid rejection."*

In *Hooked*, author Nir Eyal explores the question, "Why do some products capture our attention, while others flop?" Eyal uncovers the patterns that make certain apps and technologies hook us. These insights form the basis of the author's "Hook Model", a four-step process that designers can use to build addictive products.

7. Predictably Irrational: The Hidden Forces That Shape Our Decisions

"We usually think of ourselves as sitting the driver's seat, with ultimate control over the decisions we made and the direction our life takes; but, alas, this perception has more to do with our desires-with how we want to view ourselves-than with reality"

In this fascinating read, behavioral economist Dan Ariely outlines the ways people behave irrationally. From assuming that more expensive products are more effective to exploring the "power of free", Ariely demonstrates how mental shortcuts, biases, and leaps in logic often win over rational thought.

TWENTY-FOUR

5 FREE ONLINE COURSES THAT WILL HELP YOU APPLY BEHAVIORAL SCIENCE AND PSYCHOLOGY

Do you want to learn more about applying psychology and behavioral science to your experience? Not sure where to go after reading Choice Hacking and taking the course?

I've detailed some of my favorite free online courses in the list below. Each offers practical information you can begin applying right away. And the best part is, they're free!

1. An Introduction to Consumer Neuroscience & Neuromarketing, Coursera

 "How do we make decisions as consumers? What do we pay attention to, and how do our initial responses predict our final choices? To what extent are these processes unconscious and cannot be reflected in overt reports?

This course will provide you with an introduction to some of the most basic methods in the emerging fields of consumer neuroscience and neuromarketing. You will learn about the methods employed and what they mean. You will learn about the basic brain mechanisms in consumer choice, and how to stay updated on these topics. The course will give an overview of the current and future uses of neuroscience in business."

Why I recommend this course

For those who aren't familiar with Neuromarketing, this course is a great introduction to the principles of this emerging field. There's information overlap with other behavioral science fields, and you'll learn actionable science-based nuggets about how customers make decisions.

2. The Neuromarketing Toolbox, Copenhagen Business School via Coursera

 "Doing marketing research by asking people has been a common method and does still have advantages. On the other hand, if you want insights into the non-conscious interpretations of a consumer's decision, then you need other research tools in your research toolbox. Neuromarketing makes use of such an extended toolbox, containing both technical equipment and ways of doing experimental research.

The goal for this course is to give you an overview of this fast developing toolbox ranging from simple web-camera, to eye-tracking, and to complicated brain-scanners.

The course guides you through a contemporary literature review, giving you insights into the last decades of development within this field of research."

Why I recommend this course

This class is very actionable. I found myself revisiting the information in this course at least twice a month, in order to apply it to an experience challenge.

It's not critical, in my opinion, to complete this class from start to finish. I found it very helpful to jump around the material and take the bits I needed. However, I'm also someone who has a solid foundation in neuromarketing (and uses the tools and principles every day), so your mileage may vary.

3. Behavioral Economics in Action, University of Toronto via edX

 "How can we get people to save more money, eat healthy foods and engage in healthy behaviors, and more generally make better choices? There has been a lot written about the fact that human beings do not process information and make decisions in an optimal fashion.

This course builds on much of the fascinating work in the area of the behavioral sciences and allows the student to develop a hands-on approach by learning its methods and more importantly, how it can be

harnessed by suitably designing contexts to "nudge" choice."

Why I recommend this course

"Behavioral Economics in Action" has three main sections: principles, methods, and applications. "Principles" provides a solid foundation of nudging knowledge, and "Applications" is a great introduction to a process for designing your own nudges.

In particular, I found the "Methods" section of this course to be very helpful — it focuses on experimental design, and introduces students to actionable information about creating tests in the lab or in the field.

4. Buyer Behavior and Analysis, Curtain University via edX

 "In this course, you will learn about the role of consumer behavior within marketing. We will discuss how this behavior is shaped by the social and cultural environment, as well as a number of psychological factors.

You will learn about decision-making processes in consumption behavior in different buying situations. This will develop your ability to integrate marketing processes at a higher level.

Concepts drawn from various disciplines such as psychology, economics, and anthropology will be examined."

Why I recommend this course

This course takes behavioral science and psychology up a level, to concentrate on how culture, personality, and lifestyle affect customer decisions. You'll learn how customer opinions and attitudes are formed, which will then affect the decisions they make.

Highly recommended for those looking to bridge cultural and behavioral strategy.

5. Behavioral Finance, Duke University via Coursera

 "We make thousands of decisions every day... We usually make these decisions with almost no thought, using what psychologists call "heuristics" — rules of thumb that enable us to navigate our lives. Without these mental shortcuts, we would be paralyzed by the multitude of daily choices. But in certain circumstances, these shortcuts lead to predictable errors — predictable, that is, if we know what to watch out for.

Behavioral finance is the study of these and dozens of other financial decision-making errors that can be avoided, if we are familiar with the biases that cause them.

In this course, we examine these predictable errors, and discover where we are most susceptible to them."

Why I recommend this course

It may seem strange to recommend a behavioral finance course to improve customer experience. But this class offers a wealth of examples and frameworks that can be applied to marketing and design as well.

And although this course details the heuristics that people use to make financial decisions, the case studies and principles can be easily applied to experience design. You may also find yourself making better financial decisions as a result of taking this course.

GLOSSARY OF KEY TERMS

The Anchoring Effect, or Anchoring Bias

A bias that states that people are greatly influenced by the first piece of information they see (the anchor).

Behavioral Intervention

Attempts to change behavior through the use of psychology, behavioral science, and behavioral economics principles.

Choice Architecture

Choice Architecture refers to how we present choices to a customer on a specific touchpoint. How we present these choices will have an impact on how and what customers choose.

For instance, how many products we show on a menu board, how we've priced them in relation to one another, and the language we use to frame these products.

Choice Environment

Choice Environment is sometimes used interchangably with choice architecture. However, Choice Environment is more holistic than Choice Architecture as it encompasses the entire journey.

For instance, a Choice Environment might include several points of decision, like a mobile ordering service, a self-order kiosk, and a menu at the table. While Choice Architecture refers to the specific design of a touchpoint, such as the UX of a self-order kiosk.

Choice Overload

Also known as "overchoice", it's the theory that while some choice is good, too much choice will overwhelm (and possibly scare away) customers. A well-studied phenomenon, choice overload states that people have a hard time making a choice if we are presented with too many options.

Choice Paradox

The delicate balance between too many options and not enough choice. Coined by Barry Schwartz in his book *The Paradox of Choice*.

Cocktail Party Effect

The tendency for people focus on information relevant to them, specifically hearing their own name.

Cognitive Ease

Creating a state wherein it's easy for people to process information.

Cognitive Load

How much work we're asking a person's brain to take on. Things that increase cognitive load could include lots of product options, fine print that requires concentrated effort or having product options that are hard to compare. People can think, but they'd rather not as it's difficult, time-consuming, and painful. If we want to create experiences people love, we have to walk the fine line of giving enough information but not too much. Like the title of the famous book by digital designer Steve Krug says, "Don't make me think!".

Dan Airely

A well-regarded behavioral science researcher, Dan Airely is currently a professor at Duke University.

Ariely is the founder of the research institution The Center for Advanced Hindsight and co-founder of several companies in the behavioral economics space. He's also the author of a few New York Times Bestsellers in the behavioral science space, his most famous being *Predictably Irrational*.

Daniel Kahneman and Amos Tversky

A famous pair of research psychologists that explored the concept of dual process theory. Daniel Kahneman earned the Nobel Prize in Economics.

Decoy Effect

The idea that when people are presented with two options, they will change their preference when a third choice, the decoy, is introduced. Often companies use the decoy choice strategically, in order to guide customers toward a specific product.

Dual Process Theory

Also called Dual-system Theory, this psychological model posits that people have two systems of thinking: System 1 (automatic, fast, unconscious, and prone to bias and mental shortcuts), and System 2 (conscious, slow, and methodical).

System 1, also called "fast thinking" is our dominant way of processing information.

Endowed Progress Effect

A customer or user is more motivated to complete a task when they've already made some progress toward the goal.

Goal Gradient Effect

The tendency for to speed up their behavior to reach their goal, the closer they are to a reward. People are motivated by how much is left to reach their target, not how far they've come.

Heuristics

Heuristics are mental shortcuts that people use to avoid thinking. Also called biases, we usually aren't aware we're relying on them to make decisions.

IKEA Effect

The Ikea Effect states that people attribute more value to products they've helped create.

The Law of Small Numbers

Also called "insensitivity to sample size", this is a cognitive bias where people extrapolate from too small a sample size. Basically people make assumptions about large groups of people from the data of only a few.

Loss Aversion

People's tendency to avoid losses more than they desire equivalent gains.

Mere Exposure Effect

When people are familiar with something, they prefer it. And given a choice of two options, they'll prefer the one they've been exposed to the most (even if it's lower quality).

Operational Transparency

The inclusion of windows into a company's process so customers can see the effort that's going into their experience.

Peak-End Rule

Principle that states people judge an experience based on how they felt at its peak and its end, not the average of every moment of the experience.

Picture Superiority Effect

A psychological phenomenon wherein pictures are more likely to be remembered than words.

Priming Effect

The tendency for our brains call on unconscious connections in response to a stimulus (also called primes). Priming can change how we respond to decisions and situations by exposing us to something that triggers those unconscious connections.

Prospect Theory

An economics theory developed by Daniel Kahneman, who was awarded a Nobel prize for his work, and Amos Tversky. A founding theory of behavioral economics, it states that people decide between alternatives using reference points instead of objective outcomes.

Prospect theory postulates that people are loss averse, and will take greater risks in order to avoid a loss versus a potential gain.

Salience and Salience Bias

Salience describes the prominence or emotional resonance of an element. Salience Bias states that the brain prefers to pay attention to salient elements of an experience.

Self-reference Effect

People remember information more easily when it's relevant to them. Our brains encode personalized information differently, resulting in enhanced recall, learning, and persuasion.

Simplicity Theory

This theory states that people have a bias toward simplicity and are predisposed to choose products and experiences that minimize their cognitive load. In other words, simple experiences make people think less.

Social Proof

The tendency of people to look to the actions of others to gain psychological permission to try something new.

Top-10 Effect

This effect states that people naturally group things into round-number groups, and everything outside of these groups is inferior. In other words, top 10 lists are incredibly salient for customers—they naturally grab people's attention.

THANK YOU!

Thank you so much for reading *Choice Hacking*! I hope you enjoyed it.

If you read the book and liked it, please consider leaving a review with your favorite book retailer or Goodreads.

Reviews are a huge help for self-published authors because it helps us get our books in front of readers we otherwise wouldn't reach. Thank you!

DON'T FORGET YOUR FREE CHOICE HACKING COMPANION COURSE

While you're reading, don't forget to check out the FREE Choice Hacking Companion Course. You can learn more and sign up at ChoiceHacking.com/CompanionCourse101.

The free course includes:

- Bonus real-life examples and use cases
- Bonus video content
- Resources and links mentioned in the book Downloadable worksheets

Tap to get free access to your bonus material now: ChoiceHacking.com/CompanionCourse101

MORE BOOKS BY JENNIFER L. CLINEHENS

CX That Sings: An Introduction to Customer Journey Mapping

Available in print, hardback and eBook formats wherever books are sold. Visit CXThatSings.com/freechapter to learn more and download the first chapter free.

- **4.5/5 star rating on Goodreads**
- Includes FREE access to online resources with large, full-color downloadable images of all example Journey Maps and Personas
- All content from the example Journey Maps and Personas is also included in the text, making it easy to see, read, and highlight important passages
- Includes access to FREE video companion course launching July 6th on CXThatSings.com

Do you know what makes your customers tick?

This book lays out, in actionable detail, the process of creating a Customer Journey Map - a visual story about how people experience your brand. A bridge between your business and its buyers, Journey Maps can empower your team to understand customer motivations, fears, and challenges.

"CX That Sings" will guide you, step-by-step, through the mapping process. You'll finish feeling ready to engage stakeholders and design a Customer Journey Map that makes an impact.

In *CX That Sings*, you'll discover:

- Actionable advice, checklists, and tactics that will make you confident to start journey mapping right away
- Customer Journey Map Examples including eCommerce, Mixed Retail and Fast-Casual Dining
- How to create user and customer personas, with examples, and a "how-to guide" for creating supporting user and customer personas
- Free bonus material, including customer experience case studies
- Free access to online resources

What readers are saying

"Very clear with lots of useful online resources."

"This is a great step by step guide that anyone can follow with some really solid logic behind why each element is important."

"This book is brilliant. It quickly made me confident that I could design a customer journey map."

━━

Selection from *CX That Sings: An Introduction to Customer Journey Mapping*

Introduction

> *"You've got to start with the customer experience and work back toward the technology, not the other way around."*
> *– Steve Jobs*

It's one of the hottest topics in business. **Customer Experience (CX)**—much like Big Data, Marketing Automation, AI, and the Blockchain—is an area that's widely discussed but not well understood.

Thought leaders without much skin in the game tout CX as a cure-all for brands. Agencies go on hiring sprees. Org charts shuffle. It all seems so sexy—so *strategic*. But when you get down to it, there's not a lot of clarity around the Customer Experience process, outputs and KPIs.

According to a recent study by Havas[1], 81% of brands could disappear tomorrow and customers wouldn't care. As shocking as that statistic may seem (to marketers), it's not surprising when you start digging into Customer Experience stats. A whopping 92% of customers in a Bain and Company survey[2] said that companies fail to deliver on basic CX promises.

And that's a big, high-stakes problem.

So if you're trying to fix your customer experience, where do you start? That's where the Customer Journey Map comes in.

Why I wrote this book

Although there are several excellent books on Customer Journey and Experience Mapping, I wasn't satisfied with the available resources. Many of these books talk about Journey Mapping at a more strategic level, but not a practical one.

Given how important customer experience and Journey Mapping are to the future of business, I felt such a guide needed to be written.

Designed to be a jumping-off point, this book introduces the language, creation process, and uses for Customer Journey Maps. It's designed to be a quick read without a lot of fluff, just the nuts and bolts of making a Journey Map happen.

In an ideal world, you will finish this book and start creating CJMs right away, while continuing to learn from other resources and your own practice. But please don't stop here. There's a whole world of content out there, and many ways to approach Journey Mapping.

The Structure of "CX That Sings"

There are three big sections in this guide - designed to help you understand the piece parts of CJMs, how to build your own, and some tips to put your map into action

1. **Understanding the Map**: Best practice, examples of customer journey maps, templates, and checklists to help you get from zero to completed map with as little pain as possible.

2. **Building the Map**: From the initial discovery workshop to final visualization and validation, you'll be guided through best practice examples, checklists, case studies, and common mistakes in customer journey mapping. Includes a section on common mental biases, working cross-functionally, and using the Journey Map to sell-in the right next steps (if you're an agency), or get support for these projects from others in your organization (if you're a product manager, brand manager, or marketing director).

3. **Using your Map**: Learn how to use this as a jumping off point to develop additional opportunities, solutions, product and experience innovations, and build relationships that get CX initiatives funded, tested, completed, and measured.

In each chapter, I've included easy-to-scan sections like **Key Terms and Definitions**, **What You Need to**

Remember, Further Reading, Links, and Additional Resources.

A quick note on Journey Mapping

Despite what some people might say, there's no one way to create a Customer Journey Map. This book aims to distill fundamental guiding principals. You may find that your approach will vary slightly from mine.

That's great - you do you! But like learning to be a musician, you have to absorb the fundamentals before you can improvise. Consider this guide your introduction to the notes, rhythms, and scales of Journey Mapping. Where you take the melody is up to you.

Who was this book written for?

In writing this guide, I've assumed zero prior knowledge of a wide range of subjects: advertising, communications design, behavioral psychology, qualitative research, data analysis, and design. This isn't intended to insult anyone. Instead, it's a reflection of the audience I had in mind while writing.

Although anyone should be able to read CX *That Sings* and hit the ground running, there are a few audiences that will benefit the most:

1. Brand-side marketers, product managers, and anyone else who needs to know about customer-first thinking

Meet Jane: She's a client-side marketing manager who specializes in direct communications for a large fast casual dining chain. She's in charge of creating an onboarding email campaign for the company's new mobile app.

Jane's agency suggests they put together a customer journey map to better understand the pain points these emails might address.

But Jane's a little unsure.

She has a top-tier MBA, but her marketing program didn't mention customer-focused empathy tools. Instead, her professors spent a lot of time on classic strategic frameworks like Blue Ocean, SWOT, and Porter's Five Forces.

Jane has heard of Customer Journey Mapping. She's even Googled it and seen an example or two. But she doesn't have experience in the creation process, so she's not sure what value it might provide.

The question she's asking herself is, "Why should I pay for a big, expensive piece of strategy work when we can just use common sense? Don't we already have a pretty good understanding of our customers and what they need?"

Jane will use consumer journey maps for communications planning and internal strategy development and alignment.

Her biggest challenge is, **"I've heard customer journey mapping is important... but is it valuable to me?"**

2. Agency-side strategists, designers, planners, account folks, and consultants

Meet Ben: He's an agency-side strategist who wants to better understand the process of putting together a Customer Journey Map.

As his agency evolves from being digital specialists to a

more experience-focused shop, Ben sees the writing on the wall. If he wants to keep up with where the agency, clients, and the industry are heading, he needs to learn more about the process of Customer Journey Mapping.

Ben will use Journey Maps for communications planning and strategy development. He'll also combine Journey Maps with other forms of research and data to present solutions for clients.

His biggest challenge is, **"I've heard Customer Journey Mapping is important... but how do I create one, and use it to solve my clients' challenges?"**

Chapter One: The Customer Empathy Gap

"We see our customers as invited guests to a party, and we are the hosts. It's our job every day to make every important aspect of the customer experience a little bit better."
– Jeff Bezos

Does CX Pass the ROI Test?

McKinsey & Company has performed extensive research regarding the business impact of CX.

In their analysis, they've found "companies that offer consistently best-in-class customer experiences tend to grow faster and more profitably[3]."

These CX leaders are 80% more likely to retain

customers, get more positive referrals, and they don't have to spend as much on marketing to drive growth. It's clear that an excellent customer experience has a direct impact on companies' bottom lines. But if it's so important, why do so many brands get customer experience wrong?

The story that most businesses tell themselves is that they deliver a "superior experience", according to a recent Bain & Co. study[4]. Not just a good experience. A *superior* one.

After asking companies their opinions about their experience, Bain flipped the script. They asked customers what they thought of these brands' experiences. Only 8% of customers said the brands delivered on a *basic* customer experience.

And that's the critical issue—there's a breakdown between what brands are convinced their customers think, and what customers actually think. It's more fundamental than what Bain calls the "delivery gap". It's a customer empathy gap.

Defining the Customer Empathy Gap

As soon as you join an organization, you're no longer that company's customer. You're now on a never-ending quest to find Market Orientation—the ability to see your brand from the customer's point of view.

The concept of market orientation means being in tune with who your customer is and what they think, feel, believe, and want. On the surface, this seems like it should be easy. But how many of you have sat through marketing meetings where one personal antidote—"me-search", if you will—overturns thousands of customer data points?

Where someone with nothing in common with the

customer strategizes "from the gut"? That would be fine if marketers were exactly like their customers. But they're not. According to a survey by Trinity Mirror Solutions[5], marketers are more affluent, educated, left-wing, and open to risk-taking than the general public. As someone who has worked on world-class "value brands" I can tell you that secretly lots of marketers just don't get their brand's core customers.

I've seen far too many recommendations to shift brands upmarket, rework campaigns, and invest in esoteric platforms—not because that's best for customers, but because people are marketing to themselves.

The Cognitive Bias We're All Guilty Of...

Marketers—like all humans—fall prey to the cognitive bias of "in-group favoritism". We form a specific world view, surround ourselves with an echo chamber of like-minded people, and think everyone on Earth shares the same point of view.

Because we're driven by this unconscious bias, relying on our guts in marketing is dangerous business. Marketers must make sure they're seeking out Market Orientation at every opportunity.

This is an issue you see in every industry—how you think when you're up close to a project isn't how the world views your work.

The musician and producer Brian Eno described the same effect in the music industry:

> "You're a completely different person as a maker than you are as a listener.

That's one of the reasons I so often leave the studio to listen to things.

A lot of people never leave the studio when they're making something, so they're always in that maker mode, screwdriving things in—adding, adding, adding.

Because it seems like the right thing to be doing in that room. But it's when you come out that you start to hear what you like."

—Brian Eno

It's in the never-ending quest to gain market orientation that empathy tools like the Customer Journey Map become critical. If you don't understand your customers, how can you expect them to buy your products?

To Create Empathy, Use a Customer Journey Map

The first step to creating a breakthrough CX is created by seeing through the eyes of your customers. That's where Customer Journey Maps come in. Their core purpose is acting as a visual of how people experience your brand, and the pain points that keep them from coming back. Only after understanding the experience of those who buy your products, can you hope to improve the process in a meaningful way.

NOTES

How to Design an Irrational Experience

1. Bradley, Diana. "Corona Hits Back at 'Misinformation' about Brand Damage from Coronavirus." *PR Week*, PR Week Global, 3 Mar. 2020, www.prweek.com/article/1675555/corona-hits-back-misinformation-brand-damage-coronavirus.
2. "Corona Sales Benefit from COVID-19 Pandemic - Drinks International - The Global Choice for Drinks Buyers." *Global Drinks Industry News, Analysis and Brand Updates*, drinksint.com/news/fullstory.php/aid/8781/Corona_sales_benefit_from_COVID-19_pandemic.html.
3. Ariely, Dan. *Predictably Irrational: The Hidden Forces That Shape Our Decisions.* Harper, 2010.
4. Ross, L. (1977). "The intuitive psychologist and his shortcomings: Distortions in the attribution process". In Berkowitz, L. (ed.). *Advances in experimental social psychology.* **10**. New York: Academic Press. pp. 173–220. ISBN 978-0-12-015210-0.
5. *American Psychological Association*, American Psychological Association, psycnet.apa.org/record/1972-22883-001.
6. Dilip Bhattacharjee. "Putting Behavioral Psychology to Work to Improve the Customer Experience." *McKinsey & Company*, https://www.mckinsey.com/business-functions/marketing-and-sales/our-insights/putting-behavioral-psychology-to-work-to-improve-the-customer-experience.
7. "Inside the Nudge Unit: How Small Changes Can Make a Big Difference": David Halpern: 9780753556559: Amazon.com: Books.

1. Clear: Salience Bias

1. Ingraham, Christopher. "Analysis | What's a Urinal Fly, and What Does It Have to with Winning a Nobel Prize?" *The Washington Post*, WP Company, 9 Oct. 2017, www.washingtonpost.com/news/wonk/wp/2017/10/09/whats-a-urinal-fly-and-what-does-it-have-to-with-winning-a-nobel-prize/.
2. *American Psychological Association*, American Psychological Association, psycnet.apa.org/record/1977-20305-001.

3. 6 Strategies Inspired by a Nobel Prize Winner that Will Help You Design Better Solutions – TIC Media October 19. "Three Behavioral Insights into the Aging Mind." *Behavioraleconomics.com | The BE Hub*, 9 Feb. 2018, www.behavioraleconomics.com/three-behavioral-insights-into-the-ageing-mind/.

4. Rukšėnas, R., et al. "Formal Modelling of Salience and Cognitive Load." *Electronic Notes in Theoretical Computer Science*, Elsevier, 17 Apr. 2008, www.sciencedirect.com/science/article/pii/S1571066108002120.

5. Thorndike, Anne N, et al. "A 2-Phase Labeling and Choice Architecture Intervention to Improve Healthy Food and Beverage Choices." *American Journal of Public Health*, American Public Health Association, Mar. 2012, www.ncbi.nlm.nih.gov/pubmed/22390518.

6. Kahn, Barbara E. "Using Visual Design to Improve Customer Perceptions of Online Assortments." *Journal of Retailing*, JAI, 20 Dec. 2016, www.sciencedirect.com/science/article/abs/pii/S0022435916300793.

7. "Insights from In-Store Marketing Experiments." *Insights from In-Store Marketing Experiments | Emerald Insight*, www.emerald.com/insight/content/doi/10.1108/S1548-6435201400000011005/full/html.

8. Cutler, et al. "A Meta-Analytic Review of the Weapon Focus Effect." *Law and Human Behavior*, Kluwer Academic Publishers-Plenum Publishers, 1 Jan. 1988, link.springer.com/article/10.1007/BF02352267.

9. Abrahan, Veronika Diaz, et al. "Novelty Exposure Modulates Visual and Verbal Emotional Memory: An Experimental Design with Adults." *Acta Psychologica*, North-Holland, 11 Mar. 2020, www.sciencedirect.com/science/article/abs/pii/S0001691819303324.

10. Rodriguez, Ashley. "Netflix Finally Explains Why It Recommends Titles That Seem to Have Nothing in Common." *Quartz*, Quartz, 22 Aug. 2017, qz.com/1059434/netflix-finally-explains-how-its-because-you-watched-recommendation-tool-works/.

11. Isaac, Mathew S., and Robert M. Schindler. "The Top-Ten Effect: Consumers Subjective Categorization of Ranked Lists." *Journal of Consumer Research*, vol. 40, no. 6, Jan. 2014, pp. 1181–1202., doi:10.1086/674546.

2. Clear: The Simplicity Theory

1. "#SimplicityPays." *Global Brand Simplicity Index*, simplicityindex.com/.

2. "#SimplicityPays." *Global Brand Simplicity Index*, simplicityindex.com/.

3. "#SimplicityPays." *Global Brand Simplicity Index*, simplicityindex.com/.

4. Nick Chater (1999) The Search for Simplicity: A Fundamental Cognitive Principle?, The Quarterly Journal of Experimental Psychology Section A, 52:2, 273-302, DOI: 10.1080/713755819

5. Molla, Rani. "How Netflix Is Winning More with Less Content." *Vox*, Vox, 27 Jan. 2020, www.vox.com/recode/2020/1/27/21083551/net-flix-library-titles-decline-awards.

6. Ritson, Mark. "The First Rule of Marketing Is You Are Not the Customer." *Marketing Week*, 18 July 2019, www.marketingweek.-com/2018/07/10/mark-ritson-the-first-rule-of-marketing-is-you-are-not-the-customer/.

7. Gingiss, Dan. "How To 'Do Simple Better' In Your Customer Experience." *Forbes*, Forbes Magazine, 21 Mar. 2018, www.forbes.-com/sites/dangingiss/2018/03/21/how-to-do-simple-better-in-your-customer-experience/#3a02a76c7204.

3. Clear: Choice Overload and the Choice Paradox

1. Iyengar, Sheena S., and Mark R. Lepper. "When Choice Is Demotivating: Can One Desire Too Much of a Good Thing?" *The Construction of Preference*, pp. 300–322., doi:10.1017/cbo9780511618031.017.

2. Scheibehenne, Benjamin. "The Effect of Having Too Much Choice." 2008, https://www.researchgate.net/publication/279829979_The_effect_of_having_too_much_choice.

3. Toffler, A. *Future Shock*. Bantam Books, 1970.

4. "2019 Online Shopping Habits and Retailer Strategies." *Episerver*, https://www.episerver.com/learn/guides/2019-online-shopping-habits-and-retailer-strategies/.

5. Schwartz, Barry. *The Paradox of Choice: Why More Is Less*. Ecco, an Imprint of HarperCollins Publishers, 2016.

6. Rubin, Gretchen. *The Happiness Project*. Harper Collins USA, 2016.

7. Schwartz, Barry, and Andrew Ward. "Maximizing Versus Satisficing: Happiness Is a Matter of Choice." *Journal of Personality and Social Psychology*, 2002, doi:0022-3514.83.5.1178.

8. Joseph, Stephen. *Positive Psychology in Practice*. John Wiley & Sons, 2014.

9. Schwartz, Barry. *The Paradox of Choice: Why More Is Less*. Ecco, an Imprint of HarperCollins Publishers, 2016.

10. "The Paradox of Choice Revisited." *New Neuromarketing*, https://www.newneuromarketing.com/the-paradox-of-choice-revisited.

11. Inbar, Yoel & Botti, Simona & Hanko, Karlene. (2011). Decision speed and choice regret: When haste feels like waste. Journal of Experimental Social Psychology - J EXP SOC PSYCHOL. 47. 533-540. 10.1016/j.jesp.2011.01.011.

4. Holistic: The Mere Exposure Effect

1. Story, Louise. "Anywhere the Eye Can See, It's Likely to See an Ad." *The New York Times*, The New York Times, 15 Jan. 2007, https://www.nytimes.com/2007/01/15/business/media/15everywhere.html.
2. "Mere-Exposure Effect." *Wikipedia*, Wikimedia Foundation, 18 Dec. 2019, https://en.wikipedia.org/wiki/Mere-exposure_effect.
3. Verrier, and Diarmuid. "Evidence for the Influence of the Mere-Exposure Effect on Voting in the Eurovision Song Contest." *Sheffield Hallam University Research Archive*, Society for Judgment & Decision Making, 1 Sept. 2012, http://shura.shu.ac.uk/7451/.
4. https://en.m.wikipedia.org/wiki/Mere-exposure_effect#cite_note-zajonc_1980-6
5. Cooper, Joel, and Grant Cooper. "Subliminal Motivation: A Story Revisited." *Wiley Online Library*, John Wiley & Sons, Ltd (10.1111), 31 July 2006, https://onlinelibrary.wiley.com/doi/abs/10.1111/j.1559-1816.2002.tb01860.x.
6. Karremans, Johan C., et al. "Beyond Vicary's Fantasies: The Impact of Subliminal Priming and Brand Choice." *Journal of Experimental Social Psychology*, Academic Press, 30 Jan. 2006, http://www.sciencedirect.com/science/article/pii/S0022103105001496.
7. Oswald, Laura R. "The Structural Semiotics Paradigm for Marketing Research: Theory, Methodology, and Case Analysis." *Semiotica*, vol. 2015, no. 205, Jan. 2015, doi:10.1515/sem-2015-0005.

5. Holistic: The Priming Effect

1. Meyer, David E., and Roger W. Schvaneveldt. "Facilitation in Recognizing Pairs of Words: Evidence of a Dependence between Retrieval Operations." *Journal of Experimental Psychology*, vol. 90, no. 2, 1971, pp. 227–234., doi:10.1037/h0031564.
2. Butler, Sarah, and Julia Kollewe. "Tesco and Unilever Settle Marmite Dispute." *The Guardian*, Guardian News and Media, 13 Oct. 2016, www.theguardian.com/business/2016/oct/13/tesco-unilever-resolve-marmite-dispute-price-supermarket.
3. "Figure 2f from: Irimia R, Gottschling M (2016) Taxonomic Revision of Rochefortia Sw. (Ehretiaceae, Boraginales). Biodiversity Data Journal 4: e7720. Https://Doi.org/10.3897/BDJ.4.e7720." doi:10.3897/bdj.4.e7720.figure2f.
4. *American Psychological Association*, American Psychological Association, psycnet.apa.org/record/2008-07320-004.

5. Latu, Ioana M., et al. "Successful Female Leaders Empower Women's Behavior in Leadership Tasks." *Journal of Experimental Social Psychology*, Academic Press, 16 Jan. 2013, www.sciencedirect.com/science/article/abs/pii/S0022103113000206.

6. Zhong, Chen-Bo, et al. "Good Lamps Are the Best Police: Darkness Increases Dishonesty and Self-Interested Behavior - Chen-Bo Zhong, Vanessa K. Bohns, Francesca Gino, 2010." *SAGE Journals*, journals.sagepub.com/doi/abs/10.1177/0956797609360754.

7. Zhong, Chen-Bo, et al. "Good Lamps Are the Best Police: Darkness Increases Dishonesty and Self-Interested Behavior - Chen-Bo Zhong, Vanessa K. Bohns, Francesca Gino, 2010." *SAGE Journals*, journals.sagepub.com/doi/abs/10.1177/0956797609360754.

8. Holland, Rob W., et al. "Smells Like Clean Spirit: Nonconscious Effects of Scent on Cognition and Behavior - Rob W. Holland, Merel Hendriks, Henk Aarts, 2005." *SAGE Journals*, journals.sagepub.com/doi/abs/10.1111/j.1467-9280.2005.01597.x.

9. "The Sweet Smell of Success : Aromas: In a Test, Gamblers Put More Money into Slot Machines in a Pleasantly Scented Area. Will Las Vegas Gain a New Sense of Power?" *Los Angeles Times*, Los Angeles Times, 14 Oct. 1992, www.latimes.com/archives/la-xpm-1992-10-14-vw-323-story.html.

10. Kleinfield, N. R. "The Smell Of Money." *The New York Times*, The New York Times, 25 Oct. 1992, www.nytimes.com/1992/10/25/style/the-smell-of-money.html.

11. Chatterjee, Promothesh, and Randall L. Rose. "Do Payment Mechanisms Change the Way Consumers Perceive Products?" *Journal of Consumer Research*, vol. 38, no. 6, 2012, pp. 1129–1139. *JSTOR*, www.jstor.org/stable/10.1086/661730. Accessed 3 Mar. 2020.

12. Williams, Lawrence E, and John A Bargh. "Experiencing Physical Warmth Promotes Interpersonal Warmth." *Science (New York, N.Y.)*, U.S. National Library of Medicine, 24 Oct. 2008, www.ncbi.nlm.nih.gov/pmc/articles/PMC2737341/.

13. Rabelo, André L A, et al. "No Effect of Weight on Judgments of Importance in the Moral Domain and Evidence of Publication Bias from a Meta-Analysis." *PloS One*, Public Library of Science, 4 Aug. 2015, www.ncbi.nlm.nih.gov/pmc/articles/PMC4524628/.

14. Zampini, Massimiliano, and Charles Spence. "THE ROLE OF AUDITORY CUES IN MODULATING THE PERCEIVED CRISPNESS AND STALENESS OF POTATO CHIPS." *Wiley Online Library*, John Wiley & Sons, Ltd, 28 Feb. 2005, onlinelibrary.wiley.com/doi/abs/10.1111/j.1745-459x.2004.080403.x.

15. *American Psychological Association*, American Psychological Association, psycnet.apa.org/record/2015-56713-001.

16. Chivers, Tom. "What's next for Psychology's Embattled Field of Social Priming." *Nature News*, Nature Publishing Group, 11 Dec. 2019, www.nature.com/articles/d41586-019-03755-2.

6. Holistic: Confirmation Bias

1. "The Psychology of Judgment and Decision Making - PDF Free Download." *Epdf.pub*, epdf.pub/the-psychology-of-judgment-and-decision-making.html.
2. "A Mini Oral History of the Mailchimp High Five: Inside Design Blog." *Invisionapp, Inc.*, www.invisionapp.com/inside-design/oral-history-of-mailchimp-high-five/.
3. "A Mini Oral History of the Mailchimp High Five: Inside Design Blog." *Invisionapp, Inc.*, www.invisionapp.com/inside-design/oral-history-of-mailchimp-high-five/.
4. *Bloomberg.com*, Bloomberg, www.bloomberg.com/profile/company/1111807Z:LN.
5. "Holiday Inn Express Franchisees Endorse $20 Million Bathroom Makeover; Proprietary Showerheads, Cu." *Hotel*, 1 Oct. 2004, www.hotel-online.com/archives/archive-11826/.

7. Open: Operational Transparency

1. Herold, Tracy Stapp (February 6, 2015). "Top Fastest-Growing Franchises for 2015". *Entrepreneur*. Retrieved December 5,2017.
2. Buell, Ryan W. "Show Your Customers How Hard You're Working for Them." *Harvard Business Review*, 19 Nov. 2019, hbr.org/2019/03/operational-transparency.
3. Buell, Ryan W. and Choi, MoonSoo, Improving Customer Compatibility with Operational Transparency (July 26, 2019). Harvard Business School Technology & Operations Mgt. Unit Working Paper No. 20-013.
4. "Make Customers Happier with Operational Transparency." *Harvard Business Review*, 17 Jan. 2020, hbr.org/ideacast/2019/03/make-customers-happier-with-operational-transparency.
5. Buell, Ryan W., and Karen Donohue. "Creating Reciprocal Value Through Operational Transparency." *Management Science*, 23 May 2016, pubsonline.informs.org/doi/10.1287/mnsc.2015.2411.
6. LLC, Connected Bits. "311." *BOS*, 311.boston.gov/?service_id=4f389210e75084437f0001ca.
7. Boston, City of. "BOS:311." *App Store*, 21 Oct. 2009, apps.apple.com/us/app/bos-311/id330894558.

8. Yukako. "TESSEI: The 7 Minute Miracle of the Bullet Train Cleaning Crew." *Technology and Operations Management*, digital.hbs.edu/platform-rctom/submission/tessei-the-7-minute-miracle-of-the-bullet-train-cleaning-crew/.

8. Open: The Goal Gradient Effect

1. Kivetz, Ran, et al. "The Goal-Gradient Hypothesis Resurrected: Purchase Acceleration, Illusionary Goal Progress, and Customer Retention." *Journal of Marketing Research*, vol. 43, no. 1, 2006, pp. 39–58., doi:10.1509/jmkr.43.1.39.
2. Kivetz, Ran, et al. "Goal-Motivated Purchase Acceleration: Evidence and Consequences in Reward Programs." *PsycEXTRA Dataset*, 2004, doi:10.1037/e722842011-086.

9. Individual: The Cocktail Party Effect

1. "69% Of Companies Rate Personalizing the Customer Experience as Top in Priority." *V12*, 29 Dec. 1970, https://v12data.com/blog/69-companies-rate-personalizing-customer-experience-top-priority.
2. "2019 Personalization Development Study." *Customer Experience Optimization & Personalization Platform*, https://info.monetate.com/2019-personalization-study.html.
3. Infosys. "Rethinking Retail." *Rethinking Retail* , https://www.infosys.com/newsroom/press-releases/Documents/genome-research-report.pdf.
4. "Cocktail Party Effect." *Wikipedia*, Wikimedia Foundation, 18 Dec. 2019, https://en.wikipedia.org/wiki/Cocktail_party_effect.
5. Bronkhorst, Adelbert W. "The Cocktail-Party Problem Revisited: Early Processing and Selection of Multi-Talker Speech." *Attention, Perception & Psychophysics*, Springer US, July 2015, https://www.ncbi.nlm.nih.gov/pmc/articles/PMC4469089/.
6. Katie Sweet Follow @misskatiehrdy Katie Sweet. "Consumers Want Personalization: Stats Roundup." *Business 2 Community*, www.business2community.com/consumer-marketing/consumers-want-personalization-stats-roundup-01694184?
7. "2018 Personalization Development Study." *Customer Experience Optimization & Personalization Platform*, https://info.monetate.com/2018-personalization-study.html.
8. "Gartner Survey Shows Brands Risk Losing 38 Percent of Customers Because of Poor Marketing Personalization Efforts." *Gartner*, https://www.gartner.com/en/newsroom/press-releases/2019-03-11-gartner-survey-shows-brands-risk-losing-38-percent-of.

10. Individual: The Self-Reference Effect

1. Ward, Adrian F. "The Neuroscience of Everybody's Favorite Topic." *Scientific American*, Scientific American, 16 July 2013, www.scientificamerican.com/article/the-neuroscience-of-everybody-favorite-topic-themselves/.

2. Naaman, Mor, et al. "Is It Really about Me?: Message Content in Social Awareness Streams." *Is It Really about Me? | Proceedings of the 2010 ACM Conference on Computer Supported Cooperative Work*, 1 Feb. 2010, dl.acm.org/doi/10.1145/1718918.1718953.

3. "APA PsycNet." *American Psychological Association*, American Psychological Association, psycnet.apa.org/doiLanding?doi=10.1037/0022-3514.35.9.677.

4. Debevec, Kathleen, and Jean B. Romeo. "Self-Referent Processing in Perceptions of Verbal and Visual Commercial Information." *Journal of Consumer Psychology*, No Longer Published by Elsevier, 10 July 2008, www.sciencedirect.com/science/article/abs/pii/S1057740808800460.

5.

6. "Our Vision." *Dove UK*, www.dove.com/uk/stories/about-dove/our-vision.html.

7. Zed, Olivia. "How Dove's Real Beauty Campaign Won, and Nearly Lost, Its Audience." *PR Week*, PR Week Global, 17 Apr. 2019, www.prweek.com/article/1582147/doves-real-beauty-campaign-won-nearly-lost-its-audience.

8. Young, Takeshi. "Designing for Personalization: the Story of Optimizely's Homepage." *Optimizely Blog*, 28 Dec. 2018, blog.optimizely.com/2016/03/23/homepage-personalization/.

9.

11. Contextual: Defaults

1. Benartzi, S., et al. "What Happens to Workplace Pension Saving When Employers Are Obliged to Enrol Employees Automatically?" *International Tax and Public Finance*, Springer US, 1 Jan. 1970, link.springer.com/article/10.1007/s10797-019-09565-6.

2. Wang, Y., and G. Tang. "How Reference Options Affect Customer Decisions in Product Configuration." *2016 IEEE International Conference on Industrial Engineering and Engineering Management (IEEM)*, 2016, doi:10.1109/ieem.2016.7797944.

3. "Figure 2f from: Irimia R, Gottschling M (2016) Taxonomic Revision of Rochefortia Sw. (Ehretiaceae, Boraginales). Biodiversity Data Journal 4: e7720. Https://Doi.org/10.3897/BDJ.4.e7720." doi:10.3897/bdj.4.e7720.figure2f.

4. Johnson, Eric J. and Goldstein, Daniel G., Defaults and Donation Decisions (December 2004). Transplantation, Vol. 78, No. 12, pp. 1713-1716. Available at SSRN: https://ssrn.com/abstract=1323508

5. Bridgeable. "The Top 5 Behavioural Economics Principles for Designers." *Medium*, UX Planet, 26 Feb. 2018, uxplanet.org/the-top-5-behavioural-economics-principles-for-designers-ea22a16a4020.

6. "Group Report: Why and When Do Simple Heuristics Work?" *Bounded Rationality*, 2002, doi:10.7551/mitpress/1654.003.0012.

7. Daniel G. GoldsteinEric J. JohnsonAndreas HerrmannMark Heitmann. "Nudge Your Customers Toward Better Choices." *Harvard Business Review*, 30 Oct. 2014, hbr.org/2008/12/nudge-your-customers-toward-better-choices.

8. Davidai, Shai, et al. "The Meaning of Default Options for Potential Organ Donors." *Proceedings of the National Academy of Sciences of the United States of America*, National Academy of Sciences, 18 Sept. 2012, www.ncbi.nlm.nih.gov/pmc/articles/PMC3458339/.

9. Eun, Young, et al. "Social Defaults: Observed Choices Become Choice Defaults." *OUP Academic*, Oxford University Press, 11 July 2014, academic.oup.com/jcr/article/41/3/746/2907537.

10. Arthur, Charles. "Why the Default Settings on Your Device Should Be Right First Time." *The Guardian*, Guardian News and Media, 1 Dec. 2013, www.theguardian.com/technology/2013/dec/01/default-settings-change-phones-computers.

12. Contextual: The Cashless Effect

1. "Cashless Effect - We Pay More When We Can't Actually See the Money." *RSS*, www.coglode.com/gem/cashless-effect.

2. Ailawadi, et al. "The Effect of Payment Transparency on Consumption: Quasi-Experiments from the Field." *Marketing Letters*, Kluwer Academic Publishers, 1 Jan. 1998, link.springer.com/article/10.1023/A:1027444717586.

3. PRELEC, DRAZEN, and DUNCAN SIMESTER. "Always Leave Home Without It: A Further Investigation of the Credit-Card Effect on Willingness to Pay." https://web.mit.edu/simester/Public/Papers/Alwaysleavehome.pdf.

4. "Panera Launches an Unlimited Coffee Subscription." *QSR Magazine*, www.qsrmagazine.com/exclusives/panera-launches-unlimited-coffee-subscription.

5. "Panera Launches an Unlimited Coffee Subscription." *QSR Magazine*, www.qsrmagazine.com/exclusives/panera-launches-unlimited-coffee-subscription.

13. Contextual: The Anchoring Effect

1. Tversky, Amos, and Daniel Kahneman. "Judgment under Uncertainty: Heuristics and Biases." *Science*, American Association for the Advancement of Science, 27 Sept. 1974, science.sciencemag.org/content/185/4157/1124.
2. Furnham, Adrian, and Hua Chu Boo. "A Literature Review of the Anchoring Effect." *The Journal of Socio-Economics*, North-Holland, 10 Oct. 2010, www.sciencedirect.com/science/article/abs/pii/S1053535710001411.
3. Rogowtzow, Vincent, and Hockeys Estate Agents. "Consumer House Price Judgements: New Evidence of Anchoring and Arbitrary Coherence." *Taylor & Francis*, www.tandfonline.com/doi/abs/10.1080/09599916.2011.638144.
4. Streitfeld, David. "Some Online Bargains May Only Look Like One." *The New York Times*, The New York Times, 13 Apr. 2016, www.nytimes.com/2016/04/14/technology/some-online-bargains-may-only-look-like-one.html.
5. Manning, Kenneth C., and David E. Sprott. "Multiple Unit Price Promotions and Their Effects on Quantity Purchase Intentions." *Journal of Retailing*, JAI, 30 Apr. 2007, www.sciencedirect.com/science/article/abs/pii/S0022435907000334.
6. Fitzgerald, Miranda. "Aggressive Retail Discounting Could Damage Brand Reputation." *Campaign*, CampaignUK, 9 Oct. 2013, www.campaignlive.co.uk/article/aggressive-retail-discounting-damage-brand-reputation/872869.

14. Contextual: Social Proof

1. Pasternack, Alex. "The Subtle Power Of Default Choices." *Fast Company*, Fast Company, 25 Sept. 2017, www.fastcompany.com/40403706/the-subtle-power-of-default-choices.
2. Jeffries, Stuart. "Why Too Much Choice Is Stressing Us Out." *The Guardian*, Guardian News and Media, 21 Oct. 2015, www.theguardian.com/lifeandstyle/2015/oct/21/choice-stressing-us-out-dating-partners-monopolies.
3. Cialdini, Robert B. (October 2001). "Harnessing the science of persuasion". *Harvard Business Review*. **79** (9): 72–79.
4. "Recommendations From Friends Remain Most Credible Form of Advertising Among Consumers; Branded Websites Are the Second-Highest-Rated Form." *Nielsen*, www.nielsen.com/us/en/pressroom/2015/recommendations-from-friends-remain-most-credible-form-of-advertising.html.

5. Goldstein, et al. "Room with a Viewpoint: Using Social Norms to Motivate Environmental Conservation in Hotels." *OUP Academic*, Oxford University Press, 3 Mar. 2008, academic.oup.com/jcr/article/35/3/472/1856257.

6. Mollen, Saar, et al. "Healthy and Unhealthy Social Norms and Food Selection. Findings from a Field-Experiment." *Appetite*, Academic Press, 9 Feb. 2013, www.sciencedirect.com/science/article/pii/S0195666313000494.

7. "70% Of Americans Seek out Opinions before Purchasing." *Mintel*, 3 June 2015, www.mintel.com/press-centre/social-and-lifestyle/seven-in-10-americans-seek-out-opinions-before-making-purchases.

8. Cialdini, Robert B. *Influence: the Psychology of Persuasion*. Blackstone Audio, Incorporated, 2016.

9. "Recommendations From Friends Remain Most Credible Form of Advertising Among Consumers; Branded Websites Are the Second-Highest-Rated Form." *Nielsen*, www.nielsen.com/us/en/press-room/2015/recommendations-from-friends-remain-most-credible-form-of-advertising.html.

15. Contextual: Loss Aversion

1. "The Science of FOMO and What We're Really Missing Out On." *Psychology Today*, Sussex Publishers, https://www.psychologytoday.com/gb/blog/ritual-and-the-brain/201804/the-science-fomo-and-what-we-re-really-missing-out.

2. Eventbrite. "Millennials: Fueling the Experience Economy." *Https://Eventbrite-s3.s3.Amazonaws.com/Marketing/Millennials_Research/Gen_PR_Final.Pdf*, 2014.

3. "Loss Aversion." *Wikipedia*, Wikimedia Foundation, 4 Jan. 2020, https://en.wikipedia.org/wiki/Loss_aversion#cite_note-2.

4. "Loss Aversion: Behavioraleconomics.com: The BE Hub." *Behavioraleconomics.com | The BE Hub*, 18 Nov. 2019, https://www.behavioraleconomics.com/resources/mini-encyclopedia-of-be/loss-aversion/.

5. Ryan, Sean. "How Loss Aversion and Conformity Threaten Organizational Change." *Harvard Business Review*, 6 Mar. 2017, https://hbr.org/2016/11/how-loss-aversion-and-conformity-threaten-organizational-change.

6. McNeil, B J, et al. "On the Elicitation of Preferences for Alternative Therapies." *The New England Journal of Medicine*, U.S. National Library of Medicine, 27 May 1982, https://www.ncbi.nlm.nih.gov/pubmed/7070445.

7. Rubin, Karen. "The Ultimate List of Email SPAM Trigger Words." *HubSpot Blog*, https://blog.hubspot.com/blog/tabid/6307/bid/30684/the-ultimate-list-of-email-spam-trigger-words.aspx.

16. Contextual: The Decoy Effect

1. Ariely, Dan. *Predictably Irrational: The Hidden Forces That Shape Our Decisions*. Harper, 2010.
2. Shpanya, Ari. "Why Pricing Experiments Prove Our Assumptions Are Wrong." *Econsultancy*, 1 Nov. 2018, https://econsultancy.com/why-pricing-experiments-prove-our-assumptions-are-wrong/.

17. Emotional: The IKEA Effect

1. Duhigg, Charles. "The Power of Habit: Why We Do What We Do and How to Change It." *Amazon*, Doubleday Canada, 2012, www.amazon.com/Power-Habit-Why-What-Change-ebook/dp/B006WAIV6M/ref=tmm_kin_swatch_0?_encoding=UTF8&qid=1578234523&sr=8-1.
2. Prahalad, C.K., and Venkat Ramaswamy. "Co-Creation Experiences: The next Practice in Value Creation." *Journal of Interactive Marketing*, Elsevier, 13 Nov. 2009, https://www.sciencedirect.com/science/article/pii/S1094996804701073?via=ihub.
3. Norton, Michael I., et al. "The IKEA Effect: When Labor Leads to Love." *Journal of Consumer Psychology*, No Longer Published by Elsevier, 9 Sept. 2011, www.sciencedirect.com/science/article/abs/pii/S1057740811000829.
4. "Participation Brand Index." *Iris Participation Brands*, participationindex.iris-worldwide.com/.
5. "Who We Are." *HelloFresh*, https://www.hellofreshgroup.com/download/companies/hellofresh/Quarterly Reports/DE000A161408-Q2-2019-EQ-E-00.pdf.
6. Markowitz, Jaclyn. "Open Innovation at Lego – The Back Beat in 'Everything Is Awesome.'" *Technology and Operations Management*, https://digital.hbs.edu/platform-rctom/submission/open-innovation-at-lego-the-back-beat-in-everything-is-awesome/.
7. "The 'IKEA Effect': When Labor Leads to Love." *HBS Working Knowledge*, 13 Apr. 2011, https://hbswk.hbs.edu/item/the-ikea-effect-when-labor-leads-to-love.
8. "Who We Are." *Build*, https://www.buildabear.com/brand-about-story.html.
9. Park, Minjung, and Jungmin Yoo. "Benefits of Mass Customized Products: Moderating Role of Product Involvement and Fashion Innovative-

ness." *Heliyon*, Elsevier, 1 Mar. 2018, www.sciencedirect.com/science/article/pii/S2405844017321357.

18. Emotional: The Peak-End Rule

1. "Digital Transformation 2.0: Customer Experience Management." *CMO.adobe.com*, https://www.cmo.com/features/articles/2019/3/11/digital-transformation-2o-customer-experience-management.html.
2. Redelmeier, D A, and D Kahneman. "Patients' Memories of Painful Medical Treatments: Real-Time and Retrospective Evaluations of Two Minimally Invasive Procedures." *Pain*, U.S. National Library of Medicine, July 1996, https://www.ncbi.nlm.nih.gov/pubmed/8857625.
3. "Peak–End Rule." *Wikipedia*, Wikimedia Foundation, 9 Dec. 2019, https://en.wikipedia.org/wiki/Peak–end_rule.
4. "Pareto Principle." *Wikipedia*, Wikimedia Foundation, 28 Dec. 2019, https://en.wikipedia.org/wiki/Pareto_principle.
5. "ROI of Customer Experience, 2018: Qualtrics XM Institute Report." *Qualtrics*, https://temkingroup.com/product/roi-customer-experience-2018/.
6. "ROI of Customer Experience, 2018: Qualtrics XM Institute Report." *Qualtrics*, https://temkingroup.com/product/roi-customer-experience-2018/.
7. "ROI of Customer Experience, 2018: Qualtrics XM Institute Report." *Qualtrics*, https://temkingroup.com/product/roi-customer-experience-2018/.

19. How Netflix Applies C.H.O.I.C.E.

1. Binder, Matt. "Netflix Consumes 15 Percent of the World's Internet Traffic, Report Says." *Mashable*, Mashable, 4 Oct. 2018, mashable.com/article/netflix-15-percent-worlds-internet-traffic/?europe=true.
2. Watson, Amy. "Netflix Subscribers Count in the U.S." *Statista*, 22 Apr. 2020, www.statista.com/statistics/250937/quarterly-number-of-netflix-streaming-subscribers-in-the-us/.
3. Netflix Technology Blog. "Learning a Personalized Homepage." *Medium*, Netflix TechBlog, 19 Apr. 2017, netflixtechblog.com/learning-a-personalized-homepage-aa8ec670359a.
4. Netflix Technology Blog. "It's All A/Bout Testing." *Medium*, Netflix TechBlog, 19 Apr. 2017, netflixtechblog.com/its-all-a-bout-testing-the-netflix-experimentation-platform-4e1ca458c15.
5. Netflix Technology Blog. "Selecting the Best Artwork for Videos through A/B Testing." *Medium*, Netflix TechBlog, 19 Apr. 2017,

netflixtechblog.com/selecting-the-best-artwork-for-videos-through-a-b-testing-f6155c4595f6.

6. Netflix Technology Blog. "Selecting the Best Artwork for Videos through A/B Testing." *Medium*, Netflix TechBlog, 19 Apr. 2017, netflixtechblog.com/selecting-the-best-artwork-for-videos-through-a-b-testing-f6155c4595f6.

7. Netflix Technology Blog. "Selecting the Best Artwork for Videos through A/B Testing." *Medium*, Netflix TechBlog, 19 Apr. 2017, netflixtechblog.com/selecting-the-best-artwork-for-videos-through-a-b-testing-f6155c4595f6.

8. Netflix Technology Blog. "Netflix Recommendations: Beyond the 5 Stars (Part 1)." *Medium*, Netflix TechBlog, 18 Apr. 2017, netflixtechblog.com/netflix-recommendations-beyond-the-5-stars-part-1-55838468f429.

9. Netflix Technology Blog. "Netflix Recommendations: Beyond the 5 Stars (Part 1)." *Medium*, Netflix TechBlog, 18 Apr. 2017, netflixtechblog.com/netflix-recommendations-beyond-the-5-stars-part-1-55838468f429.

10. Rodriguez, Ashley. "Netflix Finally Explains Why It Recommends Titles That Seem to Have Nothing in Common." *Quartz*, Quartz, 22 Aug. 2017, qz.com/1059434/netflix-finally-explains-how-its-because-you-watched-recommendation-tool-works/.

11. Netflix Technology Blog. "Artwork Personalization at Netflix." *Medium*, Netflix TechBlog, 7 Dec. 2017, netflixtechblog.com/artwork-personalization-c589f074ad76.

12. Netflix Technology Blog. "Artwork Personalization at Netflix." *Medium*, Netflix TechBlog, 7 Dec. 2017, netflixtechblog.com/artwork-personalization-c589f074ad76.

13. awwwards. "Netflix Product Designer | Navin Iyengar | Design Like a Scientist." *YouTube*, uploaded by awwwards., 10 Aug. 2018, www.youtube.com/watch?v=XRd6Ddn4ZSY.

14. Apr, Oliver Lindberg, et al. "How Netflix Puts UX At The Heart of Design: Adobe XD Ideas." *Ideas*, 12 Apr. 2019, theblog.adobe.com/interview-with-netflix-user-experience-drives-design-ui/.

20. How Uber Applies C.H.O.I.C.E.

1.

2. "Uber." *User Experience Design Portfolio of Simon Pan*, simonpan.com/work/uber/.

3. Ambani, Priti, et al. "The Uberfication of Everything: Directory of Uber-Inspired Businesses." *Digitalwellbeingorg*, 11 Aug. 2014, digitalwellbeing.org/the-uberfication-of-everything-master-list-of-uber-inspired-businesses/.

4. Scheiber, Noam. "How Uber Uses Psychological Tricks to Push Its Drivers' Buttons." *The New York Times*, The New York Times, 2 Apr. 2017, www.nytimes.com/interactive/2017/04/02/technology/uber-drivers-psychological-tricks.html.

5. Paul, Kari. "Uber to Ban Riders with Low Ratings: Will You Pass the Test?" *The Guardian*, Guardian News and Media, 1 June 2019, www.theguardian.com/technology/2019/may/31/uber-to-ban-riders-with-low-ratings.

6. "How Is My Rating Determined?" *Uber*, help.uber.com/riders/article/how-is-my-rating-determined---?nodeId=bfea011b-3fde-4647-8b4a-5cc1bbc37899.

7. Martin, Nicole. "Uber Charges More If They Think You're Willing To Pay More." *Forbes*, Forbes Magazine, 30 Mar. 2019, www.forbes.com/sites/nicolemartin1/2019/03/30/uber-charges-more-if-they-think-youre-willing-to-pay-more/.

8. Scheiber, Noam. "How Uber Uses Psychological Tricks to Push Its Drivers' Buttons." *The New York Times*, The New York Times, 2 Apr. 2017, www.nytimes.com/interactive/2017/04/02/technology/uber-drivers-psychological-tricks.html.

9. Kamat. "How Uber Leverages Applied Behavioral Science at Scale." *Uber Engineering Blog*, 12 Aug. 2019, eng.uber.com/applied-behavioral-science-at-scale/.

10. Kamat. "How Uber Leverages Applied Behavioral Science at Scale." *Uber Engineering Blog*, 12 Aug. 2019, eng.uber.com/applied-behavioral-science-at-scale/.

21. How Disney Applies C.H.O.I.C.E.

1. Kuang, Cliff. "Disney's $1 Billion Bet on a Magical Wristband." *Wired*, Conde Nast, 3 June 2017, www.wired.com/2015/03/disney-magicband/.

2. "Inside Disney World's Secret 'Tunnels.'" *Mental Floss*, 20 Aug. 2015, www.mentalfloss.com/article/67485/inside-disney-worlds-secret-tunnels.

3. Pecho, Bruce, and Tribune. "25 SECRETS OF THE MAGIC KINGDOM." *Chicagotribune.com*, 30 Aug. 2018, www.chicagotribune.com/news/ct-xpm-1997-12-07-9712070475-story.html.

4. Ko. "Big Data Behind Disney Magic." *Digital Innovation and Transformation*, digital.hbs.edu/platform-digit/submission/big-data-behind-disney-magic/.

5. "How Disney Creates Digital Magic with Big Data." *How Disney Used Big Data*, theleadershipnetwork.com/article/disney-digital-magic-big-data.

6. Barnes, Brooks. "A Billion-Dollar Bracelet Is the Key to a Disney Park." *The New York Times*, The New York Times, 2 Apr. 2014, www.nytimes.com/2014/04/02/business/billion-dollar-bracelet-is-key-to-magical-kingdom.html.

7. Kuang, Cliff. "Disney's $1 Billion Bet on a Magical Wristband." *Wired*, Conde Nast, 3 June 2017, www.wired.com/2015/03/disney-magicband/.

8. Peters, John, et al. "Using Healthy Defaults in Walt Disney World Restaurants to Improve Nutritional Choices." *Journal of the Association for Consumer Research*, U.S. National Library of Medicine, Jan. 2016, www.ncbi.nlm.nih.gov/pmc/articles/PMC6223634/.

9. Pecho, Bruce, and Tribune. "25 SECRETS OF THE MAGIC KINGDOM." *Chicagotribune.com*, 30 Aug. 2018, www.chicagotribune.com/news/ct-xpm-1997-12-07-9712070475-story.html.

10. Ratcliff, Christopher. "How Disney Uses Social Media: Vine, YouTube, Pinterest, Instagram and More." *Econsultancy*, 13 Sept. 2018, econsultancy.com/how-disney-uses-social-media-vine-youtube-pinterest-instagram-and-more/.

11. Sklar, Marty. "Walt Disney Imagineering A.A.M. Annual Meeting." Walt Disney Imagineering A.A.M. Annual meeting. 1987.

22. Hidden Dangers of Applying Behavioral Science

1. Matousek, Mark. "United Replaced Its Performance-Based Bonus System with a Lottery - and Employees Are Furious." *Business Insider*, Business Insider, 5 Mar. 2018, https://www.businessinsider.com/united-airlines-employees-furious-about-new-bonus-system-2018-3?r=UK.

2. Joe Leech. "UX, Ethics and Having a Code of Conduct." *Joe Leech*, 20 Mar. 2015, mrjoe.uk/ux-ethics-and-having-a-code-of-conduct/.

3. Thaler, Richard H. "The Power of Nudges, for Good and Bad." *The New York Times*, The New York Times, 31 Oct. 2015, www.nytimes.com/2015/11/01/upshot/the-power-of-nudges-for-good-and-bad.html.

More books by Jennifer L. Clinehens

1. Havas Meaningful Brands Study, referenced in MediaPost article "Havas Expands 'Meaningful Brands,' Studies Role Content Plays -- Or Not"; August 2018 https://www.mediapost.com/publications/article/323024/havas-expands-meaningful-brands-studies-role-co.html

2. Bain and Company, "Closing the Delivery Gap" James Allen, Frederick F. Reichheld, Barney Hamilton and Rob Markey; 2005 http://www2.bain.com/bainweb/pdfs/cms/hotTopics/closingdeliverygap.pdf

3. McKinsey and Co. "The growth engine: Superior customer experience in insurance" by Tanguy Catlin, Ewan Duncan, Harald Fanderl, and Johannes-Tobias Lorenz. April 2016 https://www.mckinsey.com/industries/financial-services/our-insights/the-growth-engine-superior-customer-experience-in-insurance

4. Bain and Company, "Closing the Delivery Gap" James Allen, Frederick F. Reichheld, Barney Hamilton and Rob Markey; 2005 http://www2.bain.com/bainweb/pdfs/cms/hotTopics/closingdeliverygap.pdf

5. Trinity Mirror Solutions: 'Why we shouldn't trust our gut instinct' Andrew Tenzer, Ian Murray; https://www.trinitymirrorsolutions.co.uk/sites/default/files/2018-07/TMS%20Why%20We%20Shouldn%27t%20Trust%20Our%20Gut%20Instinct%20White%20Paper.pdf